Housing and Building Control Act 1984

CHAPTER 29

ARRANGEMENT OF SECTIONS

PART I

DISPOSAL OF PUBLIC SECTOR DWELLING-HOUSES AND RIGHTS OF SECURE TENANTS

Right to buy

Section
1. Extension to certain cases where landlord does not own freehold.
2. Variation of circumstances in which right does not arise.
3. Further periods to count for qualification and discount.
4. Inclusion of land let with or used for purposes of dwelling-house.
5. Repayment of discount on early disposal.
6. Notice to complete by landlord.
7. Terms of conveyance or grant.
8. Dwelling-houses in National Parks and areas of outstanding natural beauty etc.
9. Secretary of State's power to give directions as to covenants and conditions.
10. Secretary of State's power to obtain information etc.
11. Secretary of State's power to give assistance.

Right to a shared ownership lease

12. Right to be granted a shared ownership lease.
13. Notice claiming exercise of right.
14. Notice of initial contribution etc.
15. Change of landlord after notice claiming right.
16. Right to further advances.
17. Completion.

Other provisions with respect to disposals

Section
18. Recovery of service charges.
19. Vesting of mortgaged dwelling-house in local authority etc.
20. Local authority and Housing Corporation indemnities for certain mortgagees.
21. Local authority contributions towards certain mortgage costs.
22. Consent to certain voluntary disposals.
23. Covenants which must or may be imposed on certain voluntary disposals.
24. Further advances in the case of certain voluntary disposals.

Other rights of secure tenants

25. Grounds and orders for possession.
26. Assignments and other disposals of secure tenancies.
27. Rent not to increase on account of certain improvements.
28. Right to carry out repairs.
29. Heating charges.

Miscellaneous

30. Power to extend right to buy etc.
31. Dwelling-houses on public trust land.
32. Errors and omissions in notices.
33. Housing association grant.
34. Repayment of housing association grant.
35. Provisions as respects certain tenants of charitable housing associations etc.
36. Meaning of " secure tenancy ".

Supplemental

37. Transitional provisions.
38. Interpretation of Part I.

PART II

SUPERVISION OF BUILDING WORK ETC. OTHERWISE THAN BY LOCAL AUTHORITIES

Supervision of plans and work by approved inspectors

39. Giving and acceptance of an initial notice.
40. Effect of an initial notice.
41. Approved inspectors.
42. Plans certificates.
43. Final certificates.
44. Cancellation of initial notice.
45. Effect of initial notice ceasing to be in force.

Supervision of their own work by public bodies

Section
46. Giving, acceptance and effect of public body's notice.

Supplemental

47. Appeals.
48. Register of notices and certificates.
49. Offences.
50. Information, reports and returns.
51. Interpretation of Part II.

Part III

Miscellaneous Amendments Relating to Building Work

Exemptions and relaxations for public bodies

52. Exemption of local authorities etc. from procedural requirements of building regulations.
53. Power of certain public bodies to relax requirements of building regulations for their own works.

Approved documents giving practical guidance

54. Approval of documents for purposes of building regulations.
55. Compliance or non-compliance with approved documents.

Certification and reports

56. Certificates of compliance with building regulations.
57. Methods of challenging section 65 notices.

Miscellaneous

58. Charges by local authorities for performing functions relating to building regulations.
59. Amendments of enactments relating to building regulations.
60. Amendments of enactments relating to sanitation and buildings.
61. Repeal of the Building Control Act 1966.
62. Interpretation of Part III.

Part IV

Miscellaneous and General

63. Financial provisions.
64. Minor and consequential amendments.
65. Repeals.
66. Short title, commencement and extent.

SCHEDULES:

Schedule 1—Extension of right to buy to certain cases where landlord does not own freehold.
Schedule 2—Schedule inserted after Schedule 1 to 1980 Act.
Schedule 3—Terms of a shared ownership lease.
Schedule 4—Service charges in respect of certain houses.
Schedule 5—Vesting of mortgaged dwelling-house in local authority etc.
Schedule 6—Amendments of sections 104B and 104C of 1957 Act.
Schedule 7—Schedule inserted after Schedule 4 to 1980 Act.
Schedule 8—Provisions consequential upon public body's notice.
Schedule 9—Sections inserted after section 65 of the 1936 Act.
Schedule 10—Section 64(4) of the 1936 Act and section 6 of the 1961 Act, as amended.
Schedule 11—Minor and consequential amendments.
Schedule 12—Repeals.

ELIZABETH II

c. 29

Housing and Building Control Act 1984

1984 CHAPTER 29

An Act to make further provision with respect to the disposal of, and the rights of secure tenants of, dwelling-houses held by local authorities and other bodies in England and Wales; to amend the law of England and Wales relating to the supervision of building work, the building regulations, sanitation and buildings and building control; and for connected purposes. [26th June 1984]

BE IT ENACTED by the Queen's most Excellent Majesty, by and with the advice and consent of the Lords Spiritual and Temporal, and Commons, in this present Parliament assembled, and by the authority of the same, as follows:—

PART I

DISPOSAL OF PUBLIC SECTOR DWELLING-HOUSES AND RIGHTS OF SECURE TENANTS

Right to buy

1.—(1) The provisions of this section and of Schedule 1 to this Act shall have effect for the purpose of extending the right to buy conferred by Chapter I of Part I of the Housing Act 1980 (in this Part of this Act referred to as "the 1980 Act") to certain cases where the landlord does not own the freehold of the dwelling-house.

Extension to certain cases where landlord does not own freehold.
1980 c. 51.

PART I

(2) In section 1(1) of the 1980 Act (right to acquire freehold or long lease) for paragraphs (a) and (b) there shall be substituted the following paragraphs—

> "(a) if the dwelling-house is a house and the landlord owns the freehold, to acquire the freehold of the dwelling-house;
>
> (b) if the landlord does not own the freehold or (whether or not the landlord owns it) the dwelling-house is a flat, to be granted a lease of the dwelling-house; and ".

(3) At the end of section 2(3) of the 1980 Act (exceptions to right to buy) there shall be inserted the words " or has an interest sufficient to grant a lease in pursuance of this Chapter—

> (a) where the dwelling-house is a house, for a term exceeding 21 years commencing with the relevant time;
>
> (b) where the dwelling-house is a flat, for a term of not less than 50 years commencing with that time."

(4) The amendments made by this section and Schedule 1 to this Act (except paragraph 10) shall not apply where the landlord's notice under section 5(1) of the 1980 Act was served before the commencement date.

Variation of circumstances in which right does not arise.

2.—(1) Subsection (5) of section 2 of the 1980 Act (exceptions to the right to buy) shall be omitted and for paragraphs 1 and 2 of Part I of Schedule 1 to that Act (circumstances in which the right to buy does not arise) there shall be substituted the following paragraph—

> " 1.—(1) The dwelling-house either forms part of, or is within the curtilage of, a building to which sub-paragraph (2) below applies or is situated in a cemetery and (in either case) the dwelling-house was let to the tenant or to a predecessor in title of his in consequence of the tenant or predecessor being in the employment of the landlord or of a body specified in sub-paragraph (3) below.
>
> (2) This sub-paragraph applies to a building if the building or so much of it as is held by the landlord—
>
>> (a) is held mainly for purposes other than housing purposes; and
>>
>> (b) consists mainly of accommodation other than housing accommodation;
>
> and in this sub-paragraph 'housing purposes' means the purposes for which dwelling-houses are held by local authorities under Part V of the 1957 Act or purposes corresponding to those purposes.

(3) The bodies referred to in sub-paragraph (1) above are—

(a) a local authority;
(b) a development corporation;
(c) an urban development corporation within the meaning of Part XVI of the Local Government, Planning and Land Act 1980;
(d) the Commission for the New Towns;
(e) a county council;
(f) the governors of an aided school; and
(g) the Development Board for Rural Wales."

[margin: PART I]
[margin: 1980 c. 65.]

(2) For paragraphs 3 and 4 of that Part of that Schedule there shall be substituted the following paragraphs—

" 3. The dwelling-house has features which are substantially different from those of ordinary dwelling-houses and which are designed to make it suitable for occupation by physically disabled persons and either—

(a) the dwelling-house has had those features since it was constructed or, where it was provided by means of the conversion of a building, since it was so provided; or
(b) the dwelling-house is one of a group of dwelling-houses which it is the practice of the landlord to let for occupation by physically disabled persons and a social service or special facilities are provided in close proximity to the group of dwelling-houses wholly or partly for the purpose of assisting those persons.

3A. The landlord or a predecessor of the landlord has carried out, for the purpose of making the dwelling-house suitable for occupation by physically disabled persons, one or more of the following alterations, namely—

(a) the provision of not less than 7·5 square metres of additional floor space;
(b) the provision of an additional bathroom or shower-room;
(c) the installation of a vertical lift.

3B. The dwelling-house is one of a group of dwelling-houses which it is the practice of the landlord to let for occupation by persons who are suffering or have suffered from a mental disorder (within the meaning of the Mental Health Act 1983) and a social service or special facilities are provided wholly or partly for the purpose of assisting those persons.

[margin: 1983 c. 20.]

PART I

4. The dwelling-house is one of a group of dwelling-houses which are particularly suitable, having regard to their location, size, design, heating systems and other features, for occupation by persons of pensionable age and which it is the practice of the landlord to let for occupation by such persons, or for occupation by such persons and physically disabled persons, and special facilities are provided wholly or mainly for the purpose of assisting those persons which consist of or include either—

(a) the services of a resident warden; or

(b) the services of a non-resident warden, a system for calling him and the use of a common room in close proximity to the group of dwelling-houses."

(3) For paragraph 5 of that Part of that Schedule there shall be substituted the following paragraph—

" 5.—(1) The Secretary of State has determined, on the application of the landlord, that the right to buy is not to be capable of being exercised with respect to the dwelling-house; and he shall so determine if, and only if, he is satisfied that the dwelling-house—

(a) is particularly suitable, having regard to its location, size, design, heating system and other features, for occupation by persons of pensionable age; and

(b) was let to the tenant or to a predecessor in title of his for occupation by a person of pensionable age or a physically disabled person (whether the tenant or predecessor or any other person).

(2) An application for a determination under this paragraph shall be made within four weeks or, in a case falling within section 5(2) of this Act, eight weeks of the service of the notice claiming to exercise the right to buy."

(4) The amendments made by subsections (1) and (3) above shall not apply where the tenant's claim to exercise the right to buy was made before the commencement date; and the amendment made by subsection (2) above shall not apply where the landlord's notice under section 5(1) of the 1980 Act was served before that date.

Further periods to count for qualification and discount.

3.—(1) For subsections (3) to (7) of section 1 of the 1980 Act (determination of qualifying period) there shall be substituted the following subsections—

" (3) The right to buy does not arise unless the period which, in accordance with Part I of Schedule 1A to this

Act, is to be taken into account for the purposes of this subsection is a period of not less than two years.

(4) Where the secure tenancy is a joint tenancy the condition in subsection (3) above need be satisfied with respect to one only of the joint tenants."

(2) For subsection (1) of section 7 of the 1980 Act (discount) there shall be substituted the following subsections—

" (1) A person exercising the right to buy is entitled to a discount equal, subject to the following provisions of this section, to the following percentage of the price before discount, that is to say—

 (a) if the period which, in accordance with Part I of Schedule 1A to this Act, is to be taken into account for the purposes of discount is less than three years, 32 per cent. ; and

 (b) if that period is three years or more, 32 per cent. plus one per cent. for each complete year by which that period exceeds two years, but not together exceeding 60 per cent. ;

and where joint tenants exercise the right to buy, that Part of that Schedule shall be construed as if for the secure tenant there were substituted that one of the joint tenants whose substitution will produce the largest discount.

(1A) There shall be deducted from the discount any amount which, in accordance with Part II of Schedule 1A to this Act, falls to be so deducted."

(3) In subsection (2) of that section after the words " 31st March 1974 " there shall be inserted the words " (or such later date as may be specified in an order made by the Secretary of State) ".

(4) Subsections (5) to (11) of that section and section 15 of that Act (children succeeding parents) shall be omitted.

(5) After Schedule 1 to the 1980 Act there shall be inserted, as Schedule 1A, the Schedule set out in Schedule 2 to this Act.

(6) The amendments made by this section shall not apply—

 (a) for the purposes of section 1(3) of the 1980 Act where the landlord's notice under section 5(1) of that Act was served before the commencement date ; or

 (b) for the purposes of discount where the notice under section 10(1) of that Act was served before that date.

PART I
Inclusion of land let with or used for purposes of dwelling-house.

4.—(1) For the avoidance of doubt it is hereby declared that in Chapter I of Part I of the 1980 Act " dwelling-house " has the meaning given by section 50(2) of that Act as extended by section 3(4) of that Act.

(2) In subsection (2) of section 3 of the 1980 Act (land used for purposes of dwelling-house) after the words " by virtue of " there shall be inserted the words " subsection (4) below or ".

(3) For subsection (4) of that section there shall be substituted the following subsections—

" (4) There shall be treated as included in a dwelling-house any land which is or has been used for the purposes of the dwelling-house if—

(a) the tenant, by a written notice served on the landlord at any time before he exercises the right to buy, requires the land to be included in the dwelling-house ; and

(b) it is reasonable in all the circumstances for the land to be so included.

(4A) A notice under subsection (4) above may be withdrawn by a written notice served on the landlord at any time before the tenant exercises the right to buy."

(4) Where, after the service of the notice under section 10(1) of the 1980 Act, a notice under section 3(4) of that Act is served or withdrawn, the parties shall, as soon as practicable after the service or withdrawal of that notice, take all such steps (whether by way of amending, withdrawing or re-serving any notice or extending any period or otherwise) as may be requisite for the purpose of securing that all parties are (as nearly as may be) in the same position as that in which they would have been if the notice under section 3(4) had been served or withdrawn before the service of the notice under section 10(1).

Repayment of discount on early disposal.

5.—(1) In subsection (1) of section 8 of the 1980 Act (repayment of discount on early disposal) for the words " disposal falling within subsection (3) " there shall be substituted the words " relevant disposal which is not exempted by subsection (3A) ".

(2) For subsection (3) of that section there shall be substituted the following subsections—

" (3) A disposal is a relevant disposal for the purposes of this section if it is—

(a) a further conveyance of the freehold or an assignment of the lease ; or

(b) the grant of a lease or sub-lease for a term of more than twenty-one years otherwise than at a rack rent,

whether the disposal is of the whole or part of the dwelling-house; and for the purposes of paragraph (b) above it shall be assumed that any option to renew or extend a lease or sub-lease, whether or not forming part of a series of options, is exercised, and that any option to terminate a lease or sub-lease is not exercised.

(3A) A relevant disposal is exempted by this subsection if—

- (a) it is a disposal of the whole of the dwelling-house and a further conveyance of the freehold or an assignment of the lease and the person or each of the persons to whom it is made is a qualifying person;
- (b) it is a vesting of the whole of the dwelling-house in a person taking under a will or on an intestacy;
- (c) it is a disposal of the whole of the dwelling-house in pursuance of an order under section 24 of the Matrimonial Causes Act 1973 or section 2 of the Inheritance (Provision for Family and Dependants) Act 1975; 1973 c. 18. 1975 c. 63.
- (d) the property disposed of is acquired compulsorily or by a person who has made or would have made, or for whom another person has made or would have made, a compulsory purchase order authorising its compulsory purchase for the purposes for which it is acquired; or
- (e) the property disposed of is land included in the dwelling-house by virtue of section 3(4) or 50(2) of this Act.

(3B) For the purposes of subsection (3A)(a) above a person is a qualifying person in relation to a disposal if he—

- (a) is the person or one of the persons by whom it is made;
- (b) is the spouse or a former spouse of that person or one of those persons; or
- (c) is a member of the family of that person or one of those persons and has resided with him throughout the period of twelve months ending with the disposal.

(3C) Where there is a relevant disposal which is exempted by subsection (3A)(*d*) or (*e*) above—

    (*a*) the covenant required by subsection (1) above shall not be binding on the person to whom the disposal is made or any successor in title of his; and

    (*b*) that covenant and the charge taking effect by virtue of subsection (4) below shall cease to apply in relation to the property disposed of."

(3) In subsection (4) of that section for the words " specified in " there shall be substituted the words " falling within ".

(4) After that subsection there shall be inserted the following subsection—

" (4A) The landlord may at any time by written notice served on a body falling within subsection (5) below postpone the charge taking effect by virtue of subsection (4) above to any legal charge securing any amount advanced or further advanced to the tenant by that body."

(5) For subsection (5) of that section there shall be substituted the following subsections—

" (5) The bodies referred to in subsection (4)(*b*) and (4A) above are—

    (*a*) the Housing Corporation;

    (*b*) any building society;

    (*c*) any body falling within paragraphs 6 to 9 of the Schedule to the Home Purchase Assistance and Housing Corporation Guarantee Act 1978; and

    (*d*) any body specified or of a class or description specified in an order made by the Secretary of State with the consent of the Treasury.

(5A) Before making an order under subsection (5) above varying or revoking an order previously made, the Secretary of State shall give an opportunity for representations to be made on behalf of any body which, if the order were made, would cease to be a body falling within that subsection."

(6) In subsection (8) of that section for the words " disposal falling within subsection (3) above " there shall be substituted the words " relevant disposal which is not exempted by subsection (3A) above ".

(7) Where any conveyance or grant executed in pursuance of Chapter I of Part I of the 1980 Act before the commencement date contains the covenant required by section 8(1) of that Act,

then, as from that date, that covenant shall have effect with such modifications as may be necessary to bring it into conformity with the amendments made by this section.

6.—(1) In subsection (1) of section 16 of the 1980 Act (completion) for the words from " matters " to " dwelling-house " there shall be substituted the words " relevant matters ".

Notice to complete by landlord.

(2) For subsection (2) of that section there shall be substituted the following subsections—

" (2) Subject to subsections (2A) and (3) below, the landlord may at any time serve on the tenant a written notice—
  (a) requiring him—
    (i) if all relevant matters have been agreed or determined, to complete the transaction within a period stated in the notice;
    (ii) if any relevant matters are outstanding, to serve on the landlord within that period a written notice to that effect specifying those matters; and
  (b) informing the tenant of the effect of this subsection and of subsections (2A), (3), (6) and (6B) below;
and the period stated in a notice under this subsection shall be such period (not less than 56 days) as may be reasonable in the circumstances.

(2A) A notice under subsection (2) above shall not be served at any time if, at that time—
  (a) any requirement for the determination or re-determination of the value of the dwelling-house by the district valuer has not been complied with;
  (b) any proceedings for the determination of any other relevant matter have not been disposed of; or
  (c) any relevant matter stated to be outstanding in a written notice served on the landlord by the tenant has not been agreed in writing or determined."

(3) In subsection (3) of that section for the words " three months ", in each place where they occur, there shall be substituted the words " nine months ".

(4) For subsection (6) of that section there shall be substituted the following subsections—

" (6) If the tenant does not comply with a notice under subsection (2) above, the landlord may serve on him a further written notice—
  (a) requiring him to complete the transaction within a period stated in the notice; and

PART I
(b) informing him of the effect of subsection (6B) below;

and the period stated in a notice under this subsection shall be such period (not less than 56 days) as may be reasonable in the circumstances.

(6A) At any time before the end of the period stated in a notice under subsection (6) above (or that period as extended under this subsection), the landlord may by a written notice served on the tenant extend (or further extend) that period.

(6B) If the tenant does not comply with a notice under subsection (6) above the notice claiming to exercise the right to buy shall be deemed to be withdrawn at the end of the period stated in the notice under that subsection or, as the case may require, that period as extended under subsection (6A) above."

(5) In subsection (7) of that section for the words " subsection (6) " there shall be substituted the words " subsection (6B) " and in subsection (9) of that section for the words " subsection (2) " there shall be substituted the words " subsection (6) ".

(6) After subsection (11) of that section there shall be inserted the following subsection—

" (12) In this section ' relevant matters ' means matters relating to the grant and to the amount to be left outstanding or advanced on the security of the dwelling-house."

(7) Subsection (6B) of section 16 of the 1980 Act shall apply in relation to a notice under subsection (2) of that section served before the commencement date as it applies to a notice under subsection (6) of that section served after that date.

Terms of conveyance or grant.

7.—(1) Schedule 2 to the 1980 Act (conveyance of freehold and grant of lease) shall have effect, and shall be deemed always to have had effect, as if in paragraph 5 after the words " Subject to " there were inserted the words " paragraph 5A below and " and after that paragraph there were inserted the following paragraph—

" 5A. Any provision of the conveyance or lease shall be void in so far as it purports to enable the landlord to charge the tenant any sum for or in connection with the giving of any consent or approval."

(2) For the avoidance of doubt it is hereby declared—
(a) that nothing in paragraph 8 of that Schedule shall be taken as affecting the operation of paragraph 5 of that Schedule ; and

(b) that the burdens specified in paragraph 9 of that Schedule do not include burdens created by the conveyance.

(3) For paragraphs 16 and 17 of that Schedule there shall be substituted the following paragraphs—

" 16. A provision is not void by virtue of paragraph 15 above in so far as it requires the tenant to bear a reasonable part of—

(a) the costs of carrying out repairs not amounting to the making good of structural defects;

(b) the costs of making good any structural defects falling within paragraph 17 below; or

(c) where the lease acknowledges the right of the tenant and his successors in title to production of the relevant policy, the costs of insuring against risks involving such repairs or the making good of such defects.

17.—(1) A structural defect falls within this paragraph if the notice under section 10 of this Act—

(a) informed the tenant of its existence; and

(b) stated the landlord's estimate of the amount (at current prices) which would be payable by the tenant towards the costs of making it good.

(2) A structural defect falls within this paragraph if the landlord does not become aware of its existence earlier than 10 years after the lease is granted."

(4) Nothing in subsection (1) above shall entitle any person to recover a sum paid by him for or in connection with a consent or approval given before the commencement date; and the amendment made by subsection (3) above shall not apply where the notice under section 10(1) of the 1980 Act was served before that date.

8.—(1) In subsection (1) of section 19 of the 1980 Act (dwelling-houses in National Parks and areas of outstanding natural beauty etc.) for the words " and his successors in title " there shall be substituted the words " (including any successor in title of his and any person deriving title under him or any such successor) ". *Dwelling-houses in National Parks and areas of outstanding natural beauty etc.*

(2) In subsection (2) of that section for the words " his successors in title " there shall be substituted the words " a

successor in title of his" and for the words "disposal falling within subsection (8) below" there shall be substituted the words "relevant disposal which is not exempted by section 8(3A) of this Act".

(3) In subsection (4) of that section for the words "disposal falling within subsection (8) below unless" there shall be substituted the words "relevant disposal which is not exempted by section 8(3A) of this Act unless in relation to that or a previous such disposal" and for the words "(or his successor in title)" there shall be substituted the words "(or his successor in title or the person deriving title under him or his successor)".

(4) In subsection (6) of that section for the words from "it would realise" onwards there shall be substituted the words "the interest to be reconveyed or surrendered would realise if sold on the open market by a willing vendor on the assumption that any liability under the covenant required by section 8(1) of this Act would be discharged by the vendor".

(5) For subsection (7) of that section there shall be substituted the following subsection—

"(7) If the landlord accepts the offer mentioned in subsection (4) above, the consideration shall be reduced by such amount (if any) as, on a relevant disposal made at the time that the offer was made and not exempted by subsection (3A) of section 8 of this Act, would fall to be paid under the covenant required by subsection (1) of that section; and no payment shall be required in pursuance of that covenant."

(6) Subsection (8) of that section shall be omitted.

(7) For subsection (11) of that section there shall be substituted the following subsection—

"(11) Where there is a relevant disposal which is exempted by section 8(3A)(d) or (e) of this Act, any such covenant as is mentioned in subsection (1) above shall cease to apply in relation to the property disposed of."

(8) In subsection (12) of that section after the words "Secretary of State" there shall be inserted the words "and 'relevant disposal' has the same meaning as in section 8 of this Act" and for the words "disposal falling within subsection (8) above" there shall be substituted the words "relevant disposal which is not exempted by section 8(3A) of this Act".

Housing and Building Control Act 1984 c. 29

PART I

(9) Where any conveyance or grant executed in pursuance of Chapter I of Part I of the 1980 Act before the commencement date contains such a covenant as is mentioned in section 19(1) of that Act, then, as from that date, that covenant—

(a) shall be binding not only on the tenant and any successor in title of his but also on any person deriving title under him or any such successor ; and

(b) shall have effect with such modifications as may be necessary to bring it into conformity with the amendments made by this section.

9. After section 24 of the 1980 Act there shall be inserted the following sections—

Secretary of State's power to give directions as to covenants and conditions.

"Secretary of State's power to give directions as to covenants and conditions.

24A.—(1) Where it appears to the Secretary of State that, if covenants or conditions of any kind were included in conveyances or grants of dwelling-houses of any description, the conveyances or grants would not conform with Parts I and II or, as the case may be, Parts I and III of Schedule 2 to this Act, he may direct landlords generally, landlords of a particular description or particular landlords not to include covenants or conditions of that kind in conveyances or grants of dwelling-houses of that description which are executed on or after a date specified in the direction.

(2) A direction given under this section may be varied or withdrawn by a subsequent direction so given.

(3) In this section and section 24B below any reference to conveyances or grants is a reference to conveyances or grants executed in pursuance of this Chapter.

Effect of directions on existing covenants and conditions.

24B.—(1) If a direction under section 24A above so provides, the provisions of this section shall apply in relation to any covenant or condition which—

(a) was included in a conveyance or grant executed before the date specified in the direction (in this section referred to as 'the specified date') ; and

(b) could not have been so included if the conveyance or grant had been executed on or after that date.

(2) The covenant or condition shall be discharged or (if the direction so provides) modified, as from the specified date, to such extent or in such manner as

PART I

may be provided by the direction ; and the discharge or modification shall be binding on all persons entitled or capable of becoming entitled to the benefit of the covenant or condition.

(3) The landlord by whom the conveyance or grant was executed shall within such period as may be specified in the direction—

    (a) serve on the person registered as the proprietor of the dwelling-house, and on any person registered as the proprietor of a charge affecting the dwelling-house, a written notice informing him of the discharge or modification ; and

    (b) on behalf of the person registered as the proprietor of the dwelling-house, apply to the Chief Land Registrar (and pay the appropriate fee) for notice of the discharge or modification to be entered in the register ;

1925 c 21.

and for the purposes of enabling the landlord to comply with the requirements of this subsection, the Chief Land Registrar shall (notwithstanding section 112 of the Land Registration Act 1925) allow any person authorised by the landlord to inspect and make copies of and extracts from any register or document which is in the custody of the Chief Land Registrar and relates to the dwelling-house.

(4) Notwithstanding anything in section 64 of the Land Registration Act 1925, notice of the discharge or modification may be entered in the register without the production of any land certificate outstanding in respect of the dwelling-house, but without prejudice to the power of the Chief Land Registrar to compel production of the certificate for the purposes mentioned in that section."

Secretary of State's power to obtain information etc.

10. After section 24B of the 1980 Act there shall be inserted the following section—

"Secretary of State's power to obtain information etc.

24C.—(1) Where it appears to the Secretary of State necessary or expedient for the purpose of determining whether his powers under section 23, 24A or 24B above are exercisable, or for or in connection with the exercise of those powers, the Secretary of State may by notice in writing to a landlord require it—

    (a) at such time and at such place as may be specified in the notice, to produce any document ; or

(b) within such period as may be so specified or such longer period as the Secretary of State may allow, to furnish a copy of any document or supply any information;

and any officer of the landlord designated in the notice for that purpose or having custody or control of the document or in a position to give that information shall, without instructions from the landlord, take all reasonable steps to ensure that the notice is complied with.

(2) Any reference in subsection (1) above to a landlord includes a reference to—

(a) a landlord by whom a conveyance or grant was executed in pursuance of this Chapter; and

(b) a body which has become a mortgagee in consequence of the exercise by a secure tenant of the right to a mortgage."

11. After section 24C of the 1980 Act there shall be inserted the following section—

Secretary of State's power to give assistance.

"Secretary of State's power to give assistance.

24D.—(1) Where, in relation to any proceedings or prospective proceedings to which this section applies, the actual or prospective party to the proceedings who has claimed to exercise or has exercised the right to buy, or is a successor in title of a person who has exercised that right, applies to the Secretary of State for assistance under this section, the Secretary of State may grant the application if he thinks fit to do so—

(a) on the ground that the case raises a question of principle; or

(b) on the ground that it is unreasonable having regard to the complexity of the case or to any other matter, to expect the applicant to deal with the case without any assistance under this section; or

(c) by reason of any other special consideration.

(2) This section applies to any proceedings under this Chapter and any proceedings to determine any question arising under or in connection with this Chapter or any conveyance or grant executed in pursuance of this Chapter, other than proceedings to determine any question as to the value of a dwellinghouse at the relevant time.

(3) Assistance by the Secretary of State under this section may include—

(a) giving advice;

(b) procuring or attempting to procure the settlement of the matter in dispute;

(c) arranging for the giving of advice or assistance by a solicitor or counsel;

(d) arranging for representation by a solicitor or counsel, including such assistance as is usually given by a solicitor or counsel in the steps preliminary or incidental to any proceedings, or in arriving at or giving effect to a compromise to avoid or bring to an end any proceedings;

(e) any other form of assistance which the Secretary of State may consider appropriate,

but paragraph (d) above shall not affect the law and practice regulating the descriptions of persons who may appear in, conduct, defend, and address the court in, any proceedings.

(4) In so far as expenses are incurred by the Secretary of State in providing the applicant with assistance under this section, the recovery of those expenses (as taxed or assessed in such manner as may be prescribed by rules of court) shall constitute a first charge for the benefit of the Secretary of State—

(a) on any costs which (whether by virtue of a judgment or order of a court or an agreement or otherwise) are payable to the applicant by any other person in respect of the matter in connection with which the assistance is given; and

(b) so far as relates to any costs, on his rights under any compromise or settlement arrived at in connection with that matter to avoid or bring to an end any proceedings.

(5) A charge conferred by subsection (4) above is subject to any charge under the Legal Aid Act 1974 and to any provision of that Act for payment of any sum into the legal aid fund.

(6) Any expenses incurred by the Secretary of State in providing assistance under this section shall be paid out of money provided by Parliament; and

any sums received by the Secretary of State by virtue of any charge conferred by subsection (4) above shall be paid into the Consolidated Fund.

(7) Any reference in this section to a solicitor includes a reference to the Treasury Solicitor."

Right to a shared ownership lease

12.—(1) Where a secure tenant has claimed to exercise the right to buy and the conditions mentioned in subsection (2) below are satisfied, the tenant shall also have the right to be granted a shared ownership lease of the dwelling-house, that is to say a lease of the dwelling-house which—

Right to be granted a shared ownership lease.

(a) conforms with Schedule 3 to this Act; and

(b) subject to that, conforms with Parts I and III of Schedule 2 to the 1980 Act (terms of lease).

(2) The conditions referred to in subsection (1) above are—

(a) that the right to buy has been established and the tenant's notice under section 5(1) of the 1980 Act remains in force;

(b) that the tenant has claimed the right to a mortgage and the amount which the tenant is entitled, or is treated as entitled, to leave outstanding, or have advanced to him, on the security of the dwelling-house is less than the aggregate mentioned in section 9(1) of that Act; and

(c) that the tenant has, within the period of three months beginning with the service on him of the notice under section 12(4) of that Act or within that period as extended by section 16(5) of that Act, served a notice on the landlord claiming to be entitled to defer completion and has, within the same period, deposited the sum of £100 with the landlord.

13.—(1) Where a secure tenant serves on the landlord a written notice claiming to exercise the right to be granted a shared ownership lease, the landlord shall (unless the notice is withdrawn) serve on the tenant within four weeks either—

Notice claiming exercise of right.

(a) a written notice admitting the tenant's right; or

(b) a written notice denying the tenant's right and stating the reasons why, in the opinion of the landlord, the tenant does not have the right to be granted a shared ownership lease.

PART I

(2) A tenant's notice under subsection (1) above—

(a) shall state the initial share which he proposes to acquire; and

(b) may be withdrawn or varied at any time by notice in writing served on the landlord.

(3) On the service of a tenant's notice under subsection (1) above, any notice served by the landlord under subsection (2) or (6) of section 16 of the 1980 Act (notice requiring the tenant to complete the transaction in accordance with Chapter I of Part I of that Act) shall be deemed to have been withdrawn; and no notice shall be served by the landlord under the said subsection (2) or (6) whilst a tenant's notice under subsection (1) above remains in force.

(4) If, on the service by the tenant of a further notice under section 12(1) of the 1980 Act, the amount which he is entitled, or treated as entitled, to leave outstanding, or have advanced to him, on the security of the dwelling-house is equal to the aggregate mentioned in section 9(1) of that Act, the tenant shall not be entitled to exercise the right to be granted a shared ownership lease and any notice of his under subsection (1) above shall be deemed to have been withdrawn.

(5) Where a tenant's notice under subsection (1) above is withdrawn, or deemed to have been withdrawn, the tenant may, subject to subsection 16(6B) of the 1980 Act, complete the transaction in accordance with Chapter I of Part I of that Act.

Notice of initial contribution etc.

14.—(1) Where a secure tenant has claimed to exercise the right to be granted a shared ownership lease and that right has been established (whether by the landlord's admission or otherwise) the landlord shall, within eight weeks, serve on the tenant a written notice stating—

(a) the amount which, in the opinion of the landlord, should be the amount of the consideration for the grant of the lease determined in accordance with paragraph 2(1) of Schedule 3 to this Act on the assumption that his initial share is as stated in the notice under section 13(1) above;

(b) the effective discount on an acquisition of that share for that consideration determined in accordance with paragraph 6(3) of that Schedule;

(c) the provisions which, in the opinion of the landlord, should be included in the lease; and

(d) where the landlord is not a housing association, any variation in the provisions which, in the opinion of the landlord, should be contained in the deed by which the mortgage is to be effected.

(2) Where the landlord is a housing association, the landlord shall send a copy of the notice under subsection (1) above to the Housing Corporation; and the Housing Corporation shall, as soon as practicable after receiving that notice, serve on the tenant a written notice stating any variation in the provisions which, in the opinion of the Housing Corporation, should be contained in the deed by which the mortgage is to be effected.

15. Where, after a secure tenant has given notice claiming to exercise the right to be granted a shared ownership lease, the interest of the landlord in the dwelling-house passes from the landlord to another body, all parties shall be in the same position as if the other body had become the landlord before the notice was given and had been given that notice and any further notice given by the tenant to the landlord and had taken all steps which the landlord had taken.

Change of landlord after notice claiming right.

16.—(1) Where a secure tenant exercises both the right to be granted a shared ownership lease and the right to a mortgage, then, without prejudice to the provisions of section 18 of the 1980 Act, the deed by which the mortgage is effected shall, unless otherwise agreed between the parties, enable the tenant to require further sums to be advanced to him in the circumstances and subject to the limits stated in this section; and the right so conferred shall be exercisable, within three months of the tenant claiming to exercise his right to acquire an additional share, on the tenant serving written notice on the landlord or Housing Corporation.

Right to further advances.

(2) A notice under subsection (1) above may be withdrawn at any time by notice in writing served on the landlord or Housing Corporation.

(3) The amount which a tenant exercising the right to a further advance is entitled to have advanced to him is, subject to the limit imposed by this section, the amount of his additional contribution.

(4) The amount mentioned in subsection (3) above is subject to the limit that the aggregate of that amount and the amount for the time being secured by the mortgage does not exceed the amount to be taken into account, in accordance with regulations under this section, as the tenant's available annual income multiplied by such factor as, under the regulations, is appropriate to it.

(5) Where the right to a further advance belongs to more than one person the limit is that the aggregate of the amount mentioned in subsection (3) above and the amount for the time being secured by the mortgage does not exceed the aggregate of the

PART I
amounts to be taken into account in accordance with the regulations as the available annual income of each of them, after multiplying each of those amounts by the factor appropriate to it under the regulations.

(6) The Secretary of State may by regulations make provision for calculating the amount which is to be taken into account under this section as a person's available annual income and for specifying a factor appropriate to it; and the regulations—

(a) may provide for arriving at a person's available annual income by deducting from the sums taken into account as his annual income sums related to his needs and commitments, and may exclude sums from those to be taken into account as a person's annual income; and

(b) may (without prejudice to the generality of subsection (10) below) specify different amounts and different factors for different circumstances.

(7) Where the amount which a tenant is entitled to have advanced to him is reduced by the limit imposed by this section, the landlord may, if it thinks fit and the tenant agrees, treat him as entitled to have advanced to him such amount exceeding that limit but not exceeding the amount mentioned in subsection (3) above as the landlord may determine.

(8) As soon as practicable after the service on it of a notice required by subsection (1) above the landlord or Housing Corporation shall serve on the tenant a written notice stating—

(a) the amount which, in the opinion of the landlord or Housing Corporation, the tenant is entitled to have advanced to him on the assumption that the additional share is as stated in the tenant's notice under paragraph 3(1) of Schedule 3 to this Act;

(b) if greater than that amount, the amount which, in the opinion of the landlord or Housing Corporation, the tenant would be entitled to have advanced to him if the additional share were such that his total share would be 100 per cent.;

(c) how that amount or those amounts have been arrived at; and

(d) the provisions which, in the opinion of the landlord or Housing Corporation, should be contained in the deed by which the further mortgage is effected.

(9) Any power to make regulations under this section shall be exercisable by statutory instrument which shall be subject to annulment in pursuance of a resolution of either House of Parliament.

(10) Regulations under this section may make different provision with respect to different cases or descriptions of case, including different provision for different areas.

17.—(1) Where a secure tenant has claimed to exercise the right to be granted a shared ownership lease and that right has been established, then, as soon as all relevant matters have been agreed or determined, the landlord shall be bound, subject to the following provisions of this section, to make to the tenant a grant of a shared ownership lease of the dwelling-house for the appropriate term defined in sub-paragraph (2) of paragraph 11 of Schedule 2 to the 1980 Act (but subject to sub-paragraph (3) of that paragraph).

(2) Where the transaction is duly completed, the sum of £100 deposited by the tenant with the landlord shall be treated as having been paid towards the tenant's initial contribution.

(3) Subject to subsections (4) and (5) below, the landlord may at any time serve on the tenant a written notice—
- (a) requiring him—
    - (i) if all relevant matters have been agreed or determined, to complete the transaction within a period stated in the notice;
    - (ii) if any relevant matters are outstanding, to serve on the landlord within that period a written notice to that effect specifying those matters; and
- (b) informing the tenant of the effect of this subsection and of subsections (4), (5), (6) and (8) below;

and the period stated in a notice under this subsection shall be such period (not less than 56 days) as may be reasonable in the circumstances.

(4) A notice under subsection (3) above shall not be served at any time if, at that time—
- (a) any requirement for the determination or re-determination of the value of the dwelling-house by the district valuer has not been complied with;
- (b) any proceedings for the determination of any other relevant matter have not been disposed of; or
- (c) any relevant matter stated to be outstanding in a written notice served on the landlord by the tenant has not been agreed in writing or determined.

(5) A notice under subsection (3) above shall not be served before the end of the period mentioned in section 16(3)(c) of the 1980 Act.

(6) If the tenant does not comply with a notice under subsection (3) above, the landlord may serve on him a further written notice—

(a) requiring him to complete the transaction within a period stated in the notice ; and

(b) informing him of the effect of subsection (8) below ;

and the period stated in a notice under this subsection shall be such period (not less than 56 days) as may be reasonable in the circumstances.

(7) At any time before the end of the period stated in a notice under subsection (6) above (or that period as extended under this subsection), the landlord may by written notice served on the tenant extend (or further extend) that period.

(8) If the tenant does not comply with a notice under subsection (6) above, the notice claiming to exercise the right to be granted a shared ownership lease and the notice claiming to exercise the right to buy shall be deemed to have been withdrawn at the end of the period stated in the notice under that subsection or, as the case may require, that period as extended under subsection (7) above.

(9) If the tenant has failed to pay rent or any other payment due from him as a tenant for a period of four weeks after it has been lawfully demanded from him, then, while the whole or part of it remains outstanding—

(a) the landlord shall not be bound to complete ; and

(b) if a notice under subsection (6) above has been served on the tenant, the tenant shall be deemed not to comply with the notice.

(10) The duty imposed on the landlord by subsection (1) above shall be enforceable by injunction.

(11) On the grant of a shared ownership lease the secure tenancy of the dwelling-house shall come to an end and, if there is then a sub-tenancy, section 139 of the Law of Property Act 1925 shall apply as on a merger or surrender.

(12) In this section " relevant matters " means matters relating to the grant and to the amount to be left outstanding or advanced on the security of the dwelling-house.

Other provisions with respect to disposals

18.—(1) Subject to subsection (2) below, Schedule 4 to this Act shall apply in any case where—

(a) the requirements of subsection (3) below were satisfied with respect to a conveyance or grant of a dwelling-house which is not a flat within the meaning of Schedule 19 to the 1980 Act ; and *(b)* the conveyance or grant or, in the case of a conveyance which is an assignment of a lease, the lease enabled the vendor or lessor to recover from the purchaser or lessee a service charge, that is to say, an amount payable by the purchaser or lessee—

(i) which is payable, directly or indirectly, for services, repairs, maintenance or insurance or the vendor's or lessor's costs of management; and

(ii) the whole or part of which varies or may vary according to the relevant costs (within the meaning of Schedule 4 to this Act);

and in that Schedule expressions used in this section have the same meaning as in this section.

(2) Schedule 4 to this Act shall not apply to periods ending before the commencement date.

(3) The requirements of this subsection are satisfied with respect to a conveyance or grant if the vendor or lessor is one of the following bodies, namely—

(*a*) a local authority within the meaning of section 50 of the 1980 Act;

(*b*) a county council;

(*c*) the Commission for the New Towns;

(*d*) a development corporation;

(*e*) the Housing Corporation;

(*f*) a housing association falling within subsection (3)(*a*) of section 15 of the Rent Act 1977; 1977 c. 42.

(*g*) an urban development corporation within the meaning of Part XVI of the Local Government, Planning and Land Act 1980; and 1980 c. 65.

(*h*) the Development Board for Rural Wales.

(4) In this section and sections 19 and 20 below—

" conveyance " means a conveyance of the freehold or an assignment of a long lease;

" dwelling-house " includes a house within the meaning of the Housing Act 1957 (in this Part of this Act referred to as " the 1957 Act "); 1957 c. 56.

" grant " means a grant of a long lease;

" long lease " means a lease creating a long tenancy within the meaning of paragraph 1 of Schedule 3 to the 1980 Act.

19.—(1) Subject to subsection (2) below, Schedule 5 to this Act shall apply in any case where— Vesting of mortgaged dwelling-house in local authority etc.

(*a*) the requirements of section 18(3) above were satisfied with respect to a conveyance or grant of a dwelling-house;

PART I

1925 c. 20.

(b) the body by whom the conveyance or grant was executed (in that Schedule referred to as "the authority") is a mortgagee of the dwelling-house and as mortgagee has become entitled to exercise the power of sale conferred by section 101 of the Law of Property Act 1925 or by the mortgage deed; and

(c) the conveyance or grant contains a condition of the kind mentioned in section 104(6)(b) or (c) of the 1957 Act, a covenant imposing the limitation specified in section 19(4) of the 1980 Act or any other provision to the like effect and any period during which the provision has effect has not expired.

(2) Schedule 5 to this Act shall not apply where the conveyance or grant was executed before the passing of the 1980 Act.

(3) The vesting of a dwelling-house under Schedule 5 to this Act shall be treated as a relevant disposal for the purposes of section 104B of the 1957 Act or section 8 of the 1980 Act or any provision of the conveyance or grant to the like effect as the covenant required by section 104B(2) or section 8(1).

(4) Where any conveyance or grant executed before the commencement date contains both—

(a) the covenant required by section 104B(2) of the 1957 Act or section 8(1) of the 1980 Act or any other provision to the like effect; and

(b) a condition of the kind mentioned in section 104(6)(b) or (c) of the 1957 Act, a covenant imposing the limitation specified in section 19(4) of the 1980 Act or any other provision to the like effect,

the first mentioned covenant or provision shall have effect, as from that date, with such modifications as may be necessary to bring it into conformity with the provision made by subsections (1) and (3) above.

Local authority and Housing Corporation indemnities for certain mortgagees.

20.—(1) Local authorities and the Housing Corporation may, with the approval of the Secretary of State, enter into agreements with recognised bodies making relevant advances on the security of dwelling-houses whereby, in the event of default by the mortgagor, and in circumstances and subject to conditions specified in the agreements, an authority or the Corporation binds itself to indemnify the recognised body in respect of—

(a) the whole or part of the mortgagor's outstanding indebtedness; and

(b) any loss or expense falling on the recognised body in consequence of the mortgagor's default.

(2) The agreement may also, where the mortgagor is made party to it, enable or require the authority or the Corporation in specified circumstances to take a transfer of the mortgage and assume rights and liabilities under it, the recognised body being then discharged in respect of them.

(3) The transfer may be made to take effect—
   (a) on any terms provided for by the agreement (including terms involving substitution of a new mortgage agreement or modification of the existing one); and
   (b) so that the authority or the Corporation are treated as acquiring (for and in relation to the purposes of the mortgage) the benefit and burden of all preceding acts, omissions and events.

(4) The Secretary of State may under subsection (1) above approve particular agreements or give notice that particular forms of agreement have his approval; and
   (a) he may in either case make the approval subject to conditions;
   (b) he shall, before giving notice that a particular form has his approval, consult such organisations representative of recognised bodies and local authorities as he thinks expedient.

(5) In this section—
   " local authority" means a county or district council, the Greater London Council, a London borough council, the Common Council of the City of London or the Council of the Isles of Scilly;
   " recognised body" means any body specified or of a class or description specified in an order made by statutory instrument by the Secretary of State with the consent of the Treasury;
   " relevant advance" means an advance made to a person whose interest in the dwelling-house is or was acquired by virtue of a conveyance or grant with respect to which the requirements of section 18(3) above are or were satisfied.

(6) Before making an order under subsection (5) above varying or revoking an order previously made, the Secretary of State shall give an opportunity for representations to be made on behalf of any recognised body which, if the order were made, would cease to be such a body.

(7) Section 16(3) and (5) of the Restrictive Trade Practices Act 1976 (recommendations by services supply association to members) shall not apply to recommendations made to recog-

PART I

nised bodies about the making of agreements under this section, provided that the recommendations are made with the approval of the Secretary of State, which may be withdrawn at any time on one month's notice.

Local authority contributions towards certain mortgage costs.

21.—(1) A local authority may contribute towards any costs incurred by any person in connection with any legal charge which secures, or any proposed legal charge which is intended to secure, a relevant advance made or proposed to be made to him by a body specified in subsection (2) below, but only to the extent that the contribution does not exceed such amount as may be specified in an order made by the Secretary of State.

(2) The bodies referred to in subsection (1) above are—

(a) any recognised body; and

1962 c. 37.
1967 c. 31 (N.I.).

(b) any building society within the meaning of the Building Societies Act 1962 or the Building Societies Act (Northern Ireland) 1967.

(3) An order under subsection (1) above shall be made by statutory instrument which shall be subject to annulment in pursuance of a resolution of either House of Parliament.

(4) In this section expressions used in section 20 above have the same meaning as in that section.

Consent to certain voluntary disposals.

22.—(1) Except with the consent of the Secretary of State, a local authority shall not dispose of a dwelling-house to which this section applies otherwise than in pursuance of Chapter I of Part I of the 1980 Act or this Part of this Act.

(2) A dwelling-house is one to which this section applies if—

(a) it is let on a secure tenancy; or

(b) a lease of it has been granted in pursuance of Chapter I of Part I of the 1980 Act or this Part of this Act,

unless (in either case) it has been acquired or appropriated by the local authority for the purposes of Part V of the 1957 Act.

(3) A consent under this section may be given either generally to all local authorities or to any particular local authority or description of authority and either generally in relation to all dwelling-houses to which this section applies or in relation to any particular dwelling-house or description of dwelling-house to which this section applies.

(4) Any such consent may be given subject to such conditions as the Secretary of State sees fit to impose.

(5) Without prejudice to the generality of subsection (4) above, any such consent may be given subject to conditions as to the price, premium or rent to be obtained on a disposal of a dwelling-house to which this section applies, including conditions as to the amount by which, on a disposal of such a dwelling-house by way of sale or by the grant or assignment of a lease at a premium, the price or premium is to be, or may be, discounted by the local authority.

(6) Section 26(1) of the Town and Country Planning Act 1959 (power of local authorities etc. to dispose of land without consent) shall not apply to any disposal which requires a consent under this section.

1959 c. 53.

(7) If—
   (a) a local authority dispose of a dwelling-house to which this section applies ; and
   (b) the disposal is one which requires a consent under this section but is made without such a consent,
then, unless the disposal is to an individual (or to two or more individuals) and does not extend to any other dwelling-house to which this section applies, it shall be void and section 128(2) of the Local Government Act 1972 or, as the case may be, section 29 of the Town and Country Planning Act 1959 (protection of purchasers) shall not apply.

1972 c. 70.

(8) For the purposes of this section the grant of an option to purchase the freehold of, or any other interest in, a dwelling-house to which this section applies is a disposal and any consent given under this section to such a disposal extends to any disposal made in pursuance of the option.

(9) In this section " local authority " has the same meaning as in section 20 above.

23. Schedule 6 shall have effect for the purpose of making, in relation to section 104B (repayment of discount on early disposal) and section 104C (houses in National Parks and areas of outstanding natural beauty etc.) of the 1957 Act, provision corresponding to that made, in relation to sections 8 and 19 of the 1980 Act, by sections 5 and 8 above.

Covenants which must or may be imposed on certain voluntary disposals.

24.—(1) Where—
   (a) a lease of a dwelling-house granted otherwise than in pursuance of this Part of this Act contains a provision to the like effect as that required by paragraph 3 of Schedule 3 to this Act ; and
   (b) a body specified in section 18(3) above has, in the exercise of any of its powers, left outstanding or advanced any amount on the security of the dwelling-house,

Further advances in the case of certain voluntary disposals.

PART I that power shall include power to advance further amounts for the purpose of assisting the tenant to make payments in pursuance of that provision.

(2) This section shall be deemed always to have had effect.

Other rights of secure tenants

Grounds and orders for possession.

25.—(1) In Part I of Schedule 4 to the 1980 Act (grounds on which court may order possession) after ground 5 there shall be inserted the following grounds—

" *Ground 5A*

The tenancy was assigned to the tenant, or to a predecessor in title of his who is a member of his family and is residing in the dwelling-house, by an assignment made by virtue of section 37A of this Act and a premium was paid either in connection with that assignment or the assignment which the tenant or predecessor himself made by virtue of that section.

In this paragraph 'premium' means any fine or other like sum and any other pecuniary consideration in addition to rent.

Ground 5B

The dwelling-house forms part of, or is within the curtilage of, a building to which sub-paragraph (2) of paragraph 1 of Part I of Schedule 1 to this Act applies and—

(*a*) the dwelling-house was let to the tenant or a predecessor in title of his in consequence of the tenant or predecessor being in the employment of the landlord or of a body specified in sub-paragraph (3) of that paragraph ; and

(*b*) the tenant or any person residing in the dwelling-house has been guilty of conduct such that, having regard to the purpose for which the building is used, it would not be right for him to continue in occupation of the dwelling-house."

(2) In subsection (2) of section 34 of that Act (grounds and orders for possession) for the words " grounds 10 to 13 " there shall be substituted the words " grounds 9A to 13 " and in that Part of that Schedule after ground 9 there shall be inserted the following ground—

" *Ground 9A*

The dwelling-house either forms part of, or is within the curtilage of, a building to which sub-paragraph (2) of paragraph 1 of Part I of Schedule 1 to this Act applies or is situated in a cemetery and (in either case)—

(a) the landlord reasonably requires the dwelling-house for occupation as a residence for some person engaged in the employment of the landlord or of a body specified in sub-paragraph (3) of that paragraph or with whom, conditional on housing being provided, a contract for such employment has been entered into; and

(b) the dwelling-house was let to the tenant or to a predecessor in title of his in consequence of the tenant or predecessor being in the employment of the landlord or of a body so specified and the tenant or predecessor has ceased to be in that employment."

(3) After subsection (3) of that section there shall be inserted the following subsection—

" (3A) The matters to be taken into account by the court in determining whether it is reasonable to make an order on ground 13 shall include—
(a) the age of the tenant;
(b) the period during which the tenant has occupied the dwelling-house as his only or principal home; and
(c) any financial or other support given by the tenant to the previous tenant."

26.—(1) For section 37 of the 1980 Act (effect of assignment or subletting etc.) there shall be substituted the following sections—

"Assignments.

37.—(1) A tenancy to which subsection (2) below applies shall not be capable of being assigned, and if a tenancy to which subsection (3) below applies is assigned it ceases to be a secure tenancy, unless (in either case)—

(a) the assignment is made in pursuance of an order made under section 24 of the Matrimonial Causes Act 1973; or

(b) the assignment is made to a person in whom the tenancy would or might have vested by virtue of section 30 above had the tenant died immediately before the assignment, or in whom it would or might have so vested had the tenancy been a periodic tenancy; or

(c) the assignment is made by virtue of section 37A below.

Assignments and other disposals of secure tenancies.

1973 c. 18.

(2) This subsection applies to any tenancy which—
  (a) is a secure tenancy to which subsection (3) below does not apply; or
  (b) would be such a tenancy if the condition described in section 28(3) above as the tenant condition were satisfied.

(3) This subsection applies to any secure tenancy which is for a term certain and was granted before 5th November 1982.

(4) Where—
  (a) a tenancy ceases to be a secure tenancy by virtue of subsection (1) above; or
  (b) a tenancy which would be a tenancy to which subsection (3) above applies if the condition described in section 28(3) above as the tenant condition were satisfied is assigned,
the tenancy cannot become a secure tenancy.

Assignments by way of exchange.

37A.—(1) It is by virtue of this section a term of every secure tenancy that the tenant may, with the written consent of the landlord, assign the tenancy to a person to whom this subsection applies; and this subsection applies to any person who is the tenant under a secure tenancy and has the written consent of his landlord to assign the tenancy either to the first mentioned tenant or to another person to whom this subsection applies.

(2) The consent required by virtue of this section is not to be withheld except on one or more of the grounds set out in Schedule 4A to this Act and, if withheld otherwise than on one of those grounds, shall be treated as given.

(3) The landlord shall not be entitled to rely on any of the grounds set out in Schedule 4A to this Act unless, within 42 days of the tenant's application for the consent, the landlord has served on the tenant a notice specifying that ground and giving particulars of it.

(4) Where any rent lawfully due from the tenant has not been paid or any obligation of the tenancy has been broken or not performed, the consent required by virtue of this section may be given subject to a condition requiring the tenant to pay the outstanding rent, remedy the breach or perform the obligation.

(5) Except as provided by subsection (4) above, a consent required by this section cannot be given subject to a condition, and any condition imposed otherwise than as so provided shall be disregarded.

Other disposals.

37B.—(1) If the tenant under a secure tenancy parts with the possession of the dwelling-house or sub-lets the whole of it (or sub-lets first part of it and then the remainder) the tenancy ceases to be a secure tenancy.

(2) Where, on the death of the tenant, a secure tenancy is vested or otherwise disposed of in the course of the administration of his estate, the tenancy ceases to be a secure tenancy unless—

(a) the vesting or other disposal is in pursuance of an order made under section 24 of the Matrimonial Causes Act 1973 ; or

1973 c. 18.

(b) the vesting or other disposal is to a person in whom the tenancy would or might have vested by virtue of section 30 above had the tenancy been a periodic tenancy.

(3) Where—
   (a) a tenancy ceases to be a secure tenancy by virtue of this section ; or
   (b) in the case of a tenancy which would be a secure tenancy if the condition described in section 28(3) above as the tenant condition were satisfied, the tenant parts with the possession of the dwelling-house or sub-lets the whole of it (or sub-lets first part of it and then the remainder),

the tenancy cannot become a secure tenancy."

(2) After Schedule 4 to the 1980 Act there shall be inserted, as Schedule 4A, the Schedule set out in Schedule 7 to this Act.

(3) Subject to subsection (4) below, section 37 of the 1980 Act as originally enacted shall be deemed never to have applied in relation to the assignment of secure tenancies.

(4) Nothing in subsection (3) above shall affect—
   (a) in the case of a periodic tenancy, the operation of a notice to quit served on the tenant before the commencement date ;
   (b) in the case of a tenancy for a term certain, any proceedings for forfeiture in pursuance of a notice served on the tenant before that date.

PART I
Rent not to increase on account of certain improvements.

27. In section 39 of the 1980 Act (rent not to be increased on account of tenant's improvements) for paragraph (*b*) there shall be substituted the following paragraphs—

"(*b*) if he has died and on his death the tenancy vested under section 30 above, at any time whilst the person in whom the tenancy so vested is a secure tenant of that dwelling-house ; or

(*c*) if he has assigned the tenancy and the assignment was made as mentioned in paragraph (*a*) or (*b*) of section 37(1) above, at any time whilst the assignee is a secure tenant of that dwelling-house ; or

1983 c. 19.

(*d*) if the tenancy has been transferred to his spouse or former spouse by an order under paragraph 2 of Schedule 1 to the Matrimonial Homes Act 1983, at any time whilst the transferee is a secure tenant of that dwelling-house."

Right to carry out repairs.

28. After section 41 of the 1980 Act there shall be inserted the following section—

"*Other rights of secure tenants*

Right to carry out repairs.

41A.—(1) The Secretary of State may by regulations make a scheme for entitling secure tenants, subject to and in accordance with the provisions of the scheme—

(*a*) to carry out to the dwelling-houses of which they are secure tenants repairs which their landlords are obliged by repairing covenants to carry out ; and

(*b*) after carrying out the repairs, to recover from their landlords such sums as may be determined by or under the scheme.

(2) Regulations under this section may make such procedural, incidental, supplementary and transitional provision as may appear to the Secretary of State to be necessary or expedient.

(3) Without prejudice to the generality of subsection (2) above, regulations under this section—

(*a*) may provide for any question arising under the scheme to be referred to and determined by the county court ; and

(*b*) may provide that where a secure tenant makes application under the scheme his landlord's obligation under the repairing covenant shall cease to apply for such period and to such extent as may be determined by or under the scheme.

(4) In this section 'repairing covenant', in relation to a dwelling-house, means a covenant (whether express or implied) obliging the landlord to keep in repair the dwelling-house or any part of the dwelling-house."

29. After section 41A of the 1980 Act there shall be inserted the following section—

Heating charges.

"Heating charges.

41B.—(1) In this section—

'heating authority' means any of the following, namely a local authority, a development corporation, the Commission for the New Towns or the Development Board for Rural Wales, which—

(a) operates a generating station or other installation for producing heat; and

(b) supplies heat produced at that installation to any premises;

'heating charge' means an amount payable to a heating authority in respect of heat so produced and so supplied whether or not, in the case of heat supplied to premises let by the authority, it is payable as part of the rent;

'heating costs' means expenses incurred by a heating authority in operating a generating station or other installation for producing heat;

and a secure tenant is one to whom this section applies if a heating authority supplies heat produced at such an installation to the dwelling-house of which he is such a tenant.

(2) The Secretary of State may by regulations require heating authorities to adopt such methods for determining any heating charges payable by secure tenants to whom this section applies as will secure that the proportion of heating costs borne by each of those tenants is no greater than is reasonable.

(3) The Secretary of State may by regulations make provision for entitling secure tenants to whom this section applies, subject to and in accordance with the regulations, to require the heating authorities concerned—

(a) to furnish to them, in such form as may be prescribed by the regulations, such information as to heating charges and heating costs as may be so prescribed ; and

(b) where any such information has been so furnished, to afford them reasonable facilities for inspecting the accounts, receipts and other documents supporting the information and for taking copies or extracts from them.

(4) Regulations under this section may make such procedural, incidental, supplementary and transitional provision as may appear to the Secretary of State to be necessary or expedient.

(5) Without prejudice to the generality of subsection (4) above, regulations under this section may provide for any question arising under the regulations to be referred to and determined by the county court.

(6) Any reference in this section to heat produced at an installation includes a reference to steam produced from, and air and water heated by, heat so produced."

Miscellaneous

Power to extend right to buy etc.

30.—(1) The Secretary of State may by order provide that, in cases falling within subsection (2) below, Part I of the 1980 Act and this Part of this Act shall have effect with such modifications as are specified in the order.

(2) The cases referred to in subsection (1) above are cases where there are in a dwelling-house let on a secure tenancy one or more interests to which this subsection applies ; and this subsection applies to any interest which—

(a) is held by a body mentioned in section 18(3) above ; and
(b) is immediately superior to the interest of the landlord or to another interest to which this subsection applies.

(3) An order under this section may make different provision with respect to different cases or descriptions of case and may contain such consequential, supplementary or transitional provisions as appear to the Secretary of State to be necessary or expedient.

(4) The power to make an order under this section shall be exercisable by statutory instrument which shall be subject to annulment in pursuance of a resolution of either House of Parliament.

31. Where a dwelling-house let on a secure tenancy is land held—

(a) for the purposes of section 164 of the Public Health Act 1875 (pleasure grounds); or

(b) in accordance with section 10 of the Open Spaces Act 1906 (duty of local authority to maintain open spaces and burial grounds),

then, for the purpose of Chapter I of Part I of the 1980 Act and this Part of this Act, the dwelling-house shall be deemed to be freed from any trust arising solely by virtue of its being land held in trust for enjoyment by the public in accordance with the said section 164 or, as the case may be, the said section 10.

PART I

Dwelling-houses on public trust land.
1875 c. 55.
1906 c. 25.

32.—(1) A notice served by a tenant under Chapter I of Part I of the 1980 Act or this Part of this Act shall not be invalidated by any error in or omission from any particulars which are required by regulations under section 22 of that Act to be contained in the notice.

Errors and omissions in notices.

(2) Where as a result of any such error or omission—

(a) the landlord has mistakenly admitted or denied the right to buy in a notice under section 5(1) of the 1980 Act or the right to be granted a shared ownership lease in a notice under section 13(1) above; or

(b) the landlord or the Housing Corporation has formed a mistaken opinion as to any matter required to be stated in a notice by any of the provisions specified in subsection (3) below and has stated that opinion in the notice,

the parties shall, as soon as practicable after they become aware of the mistake, take all such steps (whether by way of amending, withdrawing or re-serving any notice or extending any period or otherwise) as may be requisite for the purpose of securing that all parties are (as nearly as may be) in the same position as that in which they would have been if the mistake had not been made.

(3) The said provisions are—

(a) section 10(1)(a) of the 1980 Act (notice of purchase price);

(b) section 12(4)(a) of that Act (notice of mortgage entitlement);

(c) section 14(1)(a) above (notice of initial contribution);

(d) section 16(8) above (notice of entitlement to further advance); and

(e) paragraph 3(4)(a) of Schedule 3 to this Act (notice of additional contribution).

B 4

(4) Subsection (2) above shall not apply in any case where the tenant has exercised the right to which the notice relates before the commencement date or before the parties become aware of the mistake.

Housing association grant.
1974 c. 44.

33.—(1) The Secretary of State may pay housing association grant under section 29 of the Housing Act 1974 (in this Part of this Act referred to as " the 1974 Act ") to an association registered under section 13 of that Act in cases where, after a tenant has exercised or has claimed to exercise the right to buy or the right to be granted a shared ownership lease, the association carries out to the dwelling-house or to the building in which it is situated works of repair or improvement.

(2) Where in a case falling within subsection (1) above a housing association grant is made after the tenant has exercised the right to buy or the right to be granted a shared ownership lease, the Secretary of State may reduce the amount of the grant.

Repayment of housing association grant.

34.—(1) In section 30(3) of the 1974 Act (repayment etc. of housing association grant in certain circumstances), after paragraph (*a*) there shall be inserted the following paragraph—

" (*aa*) there has been paid to the association in respect of any land to which the grant relates an amount payable in pursuance of—

1957 c. 56.
1980 c. 51.

(i) the covenant required by section 104B(2) of the Housing Act 1957 or section 8(1) of the Housing Act 1980 (covenant for repayment of discount) or any other provision to the like effect ; or

(ii) the provision required by paragraph 3, 6 or 7 of Schedule 3 to the Housing and Building Control Act 1984 (terms of shared ownership lease) or any other provision to the like effect ; ".

(2) If, after a housing association grant has been made under section 29 of the 1974 Act to an association registered under section 13 of that Act—

(*a*) there is such a disposal as is mentioned in paragraph (*a*) of subsection (3) of section 30 of that Act ; or

(*b*) there is made such a payment as is mentioned in paragraph (*aa*) of that subsection,

the association shall notify the Secretary of State of the disposal or payment and, if so required by written notice of the Secretary of State, shall furnish him with such particulars of and information relating to the disposal or payment as are specified in the notice.

(3) Where a housing association grant has been so made, the Chief Land Registrar may furnish the Secretary of State with such particulars and information as he may reasonably require for the purpose of determining—

(a) whether there has been such a disposal as is mentioned in paragraph (a) of subsection (3) of section 30 of the 1974 Act; or

(b) whether there has been made such a payment as is mentioned in paragraph (aa) of that subsection.

(4) The amendment made by subsection (1) above shall apply whether the payment was made before or after the commencement date.

35.—(1) This section applies to any tenant of a publicly funded dwelling-house who, but for subsection (1) or (2)(a) of section 2 of the 1980 Act (exception for cases where landlord is a charitable housing association etc.), would have the right to buy; and a dwelling-house is publicly funded for the purposes of this section if housing association grant has been paid under section 29 of the 1974 Act in respect of a project which included—

Provisions as respects certain tenants of charitable housing associations etc.

(a) the acquisition of the dwelling-house;

(b) the acquisition of a building and the provision of the dwelling-house by means of the conversion of that building; or

(c) the acquisition of land and the construction of the dwelling-house on that land.

(2) The Secretary of State may pay housing association grant under section 29 of the 1974 Act to an association registered under section 13 of that Act in cases where the association first acquires a dwelling-house and then disposes of it at a discount to a tenant to whom this section applies.

(3) Where an association registered under section 13 of the 1974 Act contracts for the acquisition of a dwelling-house and, without taking the conveyance, grant or assignment, disposes of its interest to a tenant to whom this section applies, subsection (2) above and the following provisions, namely—

(a) section 122 of the 1980 Act and sections 104B(2) to (9) and 104C of the 1957 Act as applied by that section (disposals by housing associations);

(b) Part II of Schedule 1A to the 1980 Act (qualification and discount);

(c) section 2 of the 1974 Act (consent of Housing Corporation to disposals); and

PART I

(d) section 9(2) of that Act (loans by Housing Corporation), shall have effect as if the association first acquired the dwelling-house and then disposed of it to that tenant.

(4) Section 13 of the 1974 Act shall have effect as if the additional purposes or objects mentioned in subsection (3) of that section included the purpose or object of effecting transactions falling within subsection (2) above.

(5) In this section " dwelling-house " includes a house within the meaning of the 1957 Act.

Meaning of "secure tenancy".

36.—(1) In section 28 of the 1980 Act (secure tenancies) paragraph (d) of subsection (2) and the word " or " immediately preceding that paragraph shall be omitted and after paragraph (a) of subsection (4) there shall be inserted the following paragraph—

" (aa) a county council ; ".

(2) In Schedule 3 to the 1980 Act (tenancies which are not secure tenancies) paragraph 3 shall be omitted and after paragraph 2 there shall be inserted the following paragraphs—

" 2A. A tenancy is not a secure tenancy if the tenant is a member of a police force and the dwelling-house is provided for him free of rent and rates in pursuance of regulations made under section 33 of the Police Act 1964.

1964 c. 48.

2B.—(1) A tenancy is not a secure tenancy if the tenant is an employee of a fire authority and—
 (a) his contract of employment requires him to live in close proximity to a particular fire station ; and
 (b) the dwelling-house was let to him by the authority in consequence of that requirement.

(2) In this paragraph ' contract of employment ' has the same meaning as in paragraph 2 above and ' fire authority ' means a fire authority for the purposes of the Fire Services Acts 1947 to 1959.

2C.—(1) A tenancy is not a secure tenancy until the periods to be taken into account for the purposes of this paragraph amount in aggregate to more than three years if—
 (a) within the period of three years immediately preceding the grant the conditions mentioned in paragraph 2, 2A or 2B above have been satisfied with respect to a tenancy of the dwelling-house ; and
 (b) before the grant of the tenancy the landlord notified the tenant in writing of the circumstances in which this exception applies and that in its opinion the proposed tenancy would fall within this exception.

(2) A period is to be taken into account for the purposes of this paragraph unless it is a period during which the conditions mentioned in paragraph 2, 2A or 2B above are satisfied with respect to the tenancy."

(3) In paragraph 6 of that Schedule after the words "the district or London borough", in the second and third places where they occur, there shall be inserted the words "or its surrounding area" and at the end of that paragraph there shall be added the words—

"In this paragraph 'surrounding area', in relation to a district or London borough, means the area which consists of each district or London borough that adjoins it."

(4) The paragraph inserted in Schedule 3 to the 1980 Act as paragraph 2C does not apply to a tenancy granted before the commencement date unless, immediately before that date, the interest of the landlord belongs to a county council.

(5) That paragraph and paragraphs 6 and 11 of that Schedule shall have effect in relation to a tenancy granted before the commencement date and in the case of which, immediately before that date, the interest of the landlord belongs to a county council as if for the words "before the grant of the tenancy" there were substituted the words "before the end of the period of three months beginning with the commencement of Part I of the 1984 Act".

Supplemental

37.—(1) This section applies where—

(a) a secure tenant has claimed to exercise the right to buy, that right has been established and the tenant's notice under section 5(1) of the 1980 Act remains in force on the commencement date;

(b) the tenant has claimed the right to a mortgage and the landlord or the Housing Corporation has, before the commencement date, served a notice on the tenant under section 12(4) of that Act; and

(c) the amount which, in the opinion of the landlord or Housing Corporation, the tenant is entitled to leave outstanding, or to have advanced to him, on the security of the dwelling-house is less than the aggregate mentioned in section 9(1) of that Act.

(2) The landlord shall, within four weeks of the commencement date, serve on the tenant a notice in writing informing him of the effect of this Part of this Act so far as relating to the right to be granted a shared ownership lease; and that notice shall be accompanied by a form for use by the tenant in claiming in accordance with section 13(1) above, the right to be granted a shared ownership lease.

Transitional provisions.

PART I

(3) Any notice served by the landlord under section 16(2) of the 1980 Act before the commencement date shall be deemed to have been withdrawn.

(4) No notice shall be served by the landlord under subsection (2) of section 16 of the 1980 Act earlier than, and a notice may be served by the tenant under subsection (4)(c) of that section at any time before, the expiration of the period of three months beginning with the service of the notice under subsection (2) above.

Interpretation of Part I.

38.—(1) In this Part of this Act expressions used in Chapter I of Part I of the 1980 Act have the same meanings as in that Chapter.

(2) In this Part of this Act—

1957 c. 56.
1974 c. 44.
1980 c. 51.

" the 1957 Act " means the Housing Act 1957;

" the 1974 Act " means the Housing Act 1974;

" the 1980 Act " means the Housing Act 1980;

" additional contribution " has the meaning given by paragraph 4(1) of Schedule 3 to this Act;

" additional share " shall be construed in accordance with paragraph 3 of that Schedule;

" the commencement date " means the date on which this Part of this Act comes into force;

" initial contribution " has the meaning given by paragraph 2(1) of Schedule 3 to this Act;

" initial share " shall be construed in accordance with paragraph 1 of that Schedule;

" shared ownership lease " has the meaning given by section 12(1) above;

" total share " has the meaning given by paragraph 3(9) of Schedule 3 to this Act.

PART II

SUPERVISION OF BUILDING WORK ETC. OTHERWISE THAN BY LOCAL AUTHORITIES

Supervision of plans and work by approved inspectors

Giving and acceptance of an initial notice.

39.—(1) In any cases where—

(a) a notice in the prescribed form (in the enactments relating to building regulations referred to as an " initial notice ") is given jointly to a local authority by a person intending to carry out work and a person who is an approved inspector in relation to that work;

(b) the initial notice is accompanied by such plans of the work as may be prescribed;

(c) the initial notice is accompanied by such evidence as may be prescribed that an approved scheme applies, or the prescribed insurance cover has been or will be provided, in relation to the work; and

(d) the initial notice is accepted by the local authority,

then, so long as the initial notice continues in force, the approved inspector by whom the notice was given shall undertake such functions as may be prescribed with respect to the inspection of plans of the work specified in the notice, the supervision of that work and the giving of certificates and other notices.

(2) A local authority to whom an initial notice is given—

(a) may not reject the notice except on prescribed grounds, and

(b) shall reject the notice if any of the prescribed grounds exists,

and in any case where the work to which an initial notice relates is work of such a description that, if plans of it had been deposited with the local authority, the authority could, under any enactment, have imposed requirements as a condition of passing the plans, the local authority may impose the like requirements as a condition of accepting the initial notice.

(3) Unless, within the prescribed period, the local authority to whom an initial notice is given give notice of rejection, specifying the ground or grounds in question, to each of the persons by whom the initial notice was given, the authority shall be conclusively presumed to have accepted the initial notice and to have done so without imposing any such requirements as are referred to in subsection (2) above.

(4) An initial notice shall come into force when it is accepted by the local authority, either by notice given within the prescribed period to each of the persons by whom it was given or by virtue of subsection (3) above and, subject to section 43(3) below, shall continue in force until—

(a) it is cancelled by a notice under section 44 below; or

(b) the occurrence of, or the expiry of a prescribed period of time beginning on the date of, such event as may be prescribed;

and building regulations may empower a local authority to extend (whether before or after its expiry) any such period of time as is referred to in paragraph (b) above.

(5) The form prescribed for an initial notice may be such as to require—

(a) either or both of the persons by whom the notice is

PART II

to be given to furnish information relevant for the purposes of this Part of this Act, Part II or Part IV of the 1936 Act, Part II of the 1961 Act or any provision of building regulations ; and

(b) the approved inspector by whom the notice is to be given to enter into undertakings with respect to his performance of any of the functions referred to in subsection (1) above.

(6) The Secretary of State may approve for the purposes of this section any scheme which appears to him to secure the provision of adequate insurance cover in relation to any work which is specified in an initial notice and is work to which the scheme applies.

(7) Building regulations may prescribe for the purposes of this section the insurance cover which is to be provided in relation to any work which is specified in an initial notice and is not work to which an approved scheme applies and may, in particular, prescribe the form and content of policies of insurance.

Effect of an initial notice.

40.—(1) So long as an initial notice continues in force, the function of enforcing building regulations which is conferred on a local authority by section 4(3) of the 1961 Act shall not be exercisable in relation to the work specified in the notice and, accordingly—

(a) a local authority may not give a notice under section 65(1) of the 1936 Act (removal of alteration of work which contravenes building regulations) in relation to the work so specified ; and

(b) a local authority may not institute proceedings under section 4(6) of the 1961 Act for any contravention of building regulations which arises out of the carrying out of the work so specified.

(2) For the purposes of the enactments specified in subsection (3) below,—

(a) the giving of an initial notice accompanied by such plans as are referred to in section 39(1)(b) above shall be treated as the deposit of plans ; and

(b) the plans accompanying an initial notice shall be treated as the deposited plans ; and

(c) the acceptance or rejection of an initial notice shall be treated as the passing or, as the case may be, the rejection of plans ; and

(d) the cancellation of an initial notice under section 44(5) below shall be treated as a declaration under section 66 of the 1936 Act that the deposit of plans is to be of no effect.

(3) The enactments referred to in subsection (2) above are—
   (a) subsection (2) of section 65 of the 1936 Act (powers of local authority where work is executed without plans being deposited etc.);
   (b) subsection (4) of that section (restriction of powers of local authority to act), in so far as it relates to a notice under subsection (2) thereof and to non-compliance with any such requirement as is referred to in that subsection;
   (c) subsection (5) of that section (saving for right to obtain injunction for certain contraventions), in so far as it relates to a contravention of any enactment in the 1936 Act;
   (d) section 14(6) of the Water Act 1973 (notice of proposal to erect or extend building over water authority's sewer); and 1973 c. 37.
   (e) sections 219 to 225 of the Highways Act 1980 (the advance payments code). 1980 c. 66.

(4) For the purposes of section 13 of the Fire Precautions Act 1971 (exercise of fire authority's powers where provisions of building regulations as to means of escape apply)— 1971 c. 40.
   (a) the acceptance by a local authority of an initial notice relating to any work shall be treated as the deposit of plans of the work with the authority in accordance with building regulations; and
   (b) the references in subsections (1)(ii) and (3)(b) of that section to matters or circumstances of which particulars are not or were not required by or under the building regulations to be supplied to the local authority in connection with the deposit of plans shall be construed as a reference to matters or circumstances of which particulars would not be or, as the case may be, would not have been required to be so supplied if plans were to be or had been deposited with the authority in accordance with building regulations.

41.—(1) In the enactments relating to building regulations "approved inspector" means a person who, in accordance with building regulations, is approved for the purposes of this Part of this Act— *Approved inspectors.*
   (a) by the Secretary of State; or
   (b) by a body (corporate or unincorporated) which, in accordance with the regulations, is designated by the Secretary of State for the purpose.

(2) Any such approval as is referred to in subsection (1) above may limit the description of work in relation to which the person concerned is an approved inspector.

(3) Any such designation as is referred to in subsection (1)(*b*) above may limit the cases in which and the terms on which the body designated may approve a person and, in particular, may provide that any approval given by the body shall be limited as mentioned in subsection (2) above.

(4) There shall be paid on an application for any such approval as is referred to in subsection (1) above—
  (*a*) where the application is made to the Secretary of State, such fee as may be prescribed by building regulations;
  (*b*) where the application is made to a body designated by him as mentioned in that subsection, such fee as that body may determine.

(5) Building regulations may—
  (*a*) contain provision prescribing the period for which, subject to any provision made by virtue of paragraph (*b*) or (*c*) below, any such approval as is referred to in subsection (1) above shall continue in force;
  (*b*) contain provision precluding the giving of, or requiring the withdrawal of, any such approval as is referred to in that subsection in such circumstances as may be prescribed by the regulations;
  (*c*) contain provision authorising the withdrawal of any such approval or designation as is so referred to;
  (*d*) provide for the maintenance by the Secretary of State of a list of bodies who are for the time being designated by him as mentioned in subsection (1) above and for the maintenance by the Secretary of State and by each designated body of a list of persons for the time being approved by him or them as mentioned in that subsection;
  (*e*) make provision for the supply to local authorities of copies of any list of approved inspectors maintained by virtue of paragraph (*d*) above and for such copy lists to be made available for inspection; and
  (*f*) make provision for the supply, on payment of a prescribed fee, of a certified copy of any entry in a list maintained by virtue of paragraph (*d*) above or in a copy list held by a local authority by virtue of paragraph (*e*) above.

(6) Unless the contrary is proved, in any proceedings (whether civil or criminal) a document which appears to the court to be a certified copy of an entry either in a list maintained as mentioned in subsection (5)(*d*) above or in a copy of such a list supplied as mentioned in subsection (5)(*e*) above—
  (*a*) shall be presumed to be a true copy of an entry in the current list so maintained; and
  (*b*) shall be evidence of the matters stated therein.

PART II

(7) In subsection (1) of section 62 of the 1974 Act (building regulations may require local authorities to undertake consultation in prescribed circumstances) after the words "local authorities" there shall be inserted the words "and approved inspectors".

(8) An approved inspector may make such charges in respect of the carrying out of functions referred to in section 39(1) above as may in any particular case be agreed between him and the person who intends to carry out the work in question or, as the case may be, by whom that work is being or has been carried out.

(9) Nothing in this Part of this Act prevents an approved inspector from arranging for plans or work to be inspected on his behalf by another person; but any such delegation—

(a) shall not extend to the giving of any certificate under section 42 or section 43 below; and

(b) shall not affect any liability, whether civil or criminal, of the approved inspector which arises out of functions conferred on him by this Part of this Act or by building regulations;

and, without prejudice to the generality of paragraph (b) above, an approved inspector shall be liable for negligence on the part of any person carrying out any inspection on his behalf in like manner as if it were negligence by a servant of his acting in the course of his employment.

Plans certificates.

42.—(1) Where an approved inspector—

(a) has inspected plans of the work specified in an initial notice given by him, and

(b) is satisfied that the plans neither are defective nor show that work carried out in accordance with them would contravene any provision of building regulations, and

(c) has complied with any prescribed requirements as to consultation or otherwise,

he shall, if requested to do so by the person intending to carry out the work, give a certificate in the prescribed form (in the enactments relating to building regulations referred to as a "plans certificate") to the local authority and to that person.

(2) In any case where any question arises under subsection (1) above between an approved inspector and a person who proposes to carry out any work whether plans of the work are in conformity with building regulations, that person may refer the question to the Secretary of State for his determination; and an application for a reference under this subsection shall be accompanied by such fee as may be prescribed by building regulations.

PART II

(3) Building regulations may authorise the giving of an initial notice combined with a certificate under subsection (1) above and may prescribe a single form for such a combined notice and certificate; and where such a prescribed form is used—
    (*a*) any reference in this Part of this Act to an initial notice or to a plans certificate shall be construed as including a reference to that form; but
    (*b*) should the form cease to be in force as an initial notice by virtue of subsection (4) of section 39 above, nothing in that subsection shall affect the continuing validity of the form as a plans certificate.

(4) A plans certificate—
    (*a*) may relate either to the whole or to part only of the work specified in the initial notice concerned; and
    (*b*) shall not have effect unless it is accepted by the local authority to whom it is given.

(5) A local authority to whom a plans certificate is given—
    (*a*) may not reject the certificate except on prescribed grounds; and
    (*b*) shall reject the certificate if any of the prescribed grounds exists.

(6) Unless, within the prescribed period, the local authority to whom a plans certificate is given give notice of rejection, specifying the ground or grounds in question, to—
    (*a*) the approved inspector by whom the certificate was given, and
    (*b*) the other person to whom the approved inspector gave the certificate,

the authority shall be conclusively presumed to have accepted the certificate.

(7) If it appears to a local authority by whom a plans certificate has been accepted that the work to which the certificate relates has not been commenced within the period of three years beginning on the date on which the certificate was accepted, the authority may rescind their acceptance of the certificate by notice, specifying the ground or grounds in question, given—
    (*a*) to the approved inspector by whom the certificate was given; and
    (*b*) to the person shown in the initial notice concerned as the person intending to carry out the work.

Final certificates.

43.—(1) Where an approved inspector is satisfied that any work specified in an initial notice given by him has been completed, he shall give—
    (*a*) to the local authority by whom the initial notice was accepted, and

(b) to the person by whom the work was carried out,
such certificate with respect to the completion of the work and the discharge of his functions as may be prescribed (in the enactments relating to building regulations referred to as a "final certificate").

(2) Subsections (4) to (6) of section 42 above shall have effect in relation to a final certificate as if any reference in those subsections to a plans certificate were a reference to a final certificate.

(3) Where a final certificate has been given with respect to any of the work specified in an initial notice and that certificate has been accepted by the local authority concerned, the initial notice shall cease to apply to that work, but the provisions of section 40(1) above shall, by virtue of this subsection, continue to apply in relation to that work as if the initial notice continued in force in relation to it.

44.—(1) If, at any time when an initial notice is in force— *Cancellation of initial notice.*
 (a) the approved inspector becomes or expects to become unable to carry out (or to continue to carry out) his functions with respect to any of the work specified in the initial notice, or
 (b) the approved inspector is of the opinion that any of the work is being so carried out that he is unable adequately to carry out his functions with respect to it, or
 (c) the approved inspector is of the opinion that there is a contravention of any provision of building regulations with respect to any of that work and the circumstances are as mentioned in subsection (2) below,

the approved inspector shall cancel the initial notice by notice in the prescribed form given to the local authority concerned and to the person carrying out or intending to carry out the work.

(2) The circumstances referred to in subsection (1)(c) above are—
 (a) that the approved inspector has, in accordance with building regulations, given notice of the contravention to the person carrying out the work ; and
 (b) that, within the prescribed period, that person has neither pulled down nor removed the work nor effected such alterations in it as may be necessary to make it comply with building regulations.

(3) If, at a time when an initial notice is in force, it appears to the person carrying out or intending to carry out the work specified in the notice that the approved inspector is no longer wil-

PART II

ling or able to carry out his functions with respect to any of that work, he shall cancel the initial notice by notice in the prescribed form given to the local authority concerned and, if it is practicable to do so, to the approved inspector.

(4) If any person fails without reasonable excuse to give to a local authority a notice which he is required to give by subsection (3) above he shall be liable on summary conviction to a fine not exceeding level 5 on the standard scale (as defined in section 75 of the Criminal Justice Act 1982).

1982 c. 48.

(5) If, at a time when an initial notice is in force, it appears to the local authority by whom the initial notice was accepted that the work to which the initial notice relates has not been commenced within the period of three years beginning on the date on which the initial notice was accepted, the authority may cancel the initial notice by notice in the prescribed form given—

(a) to the approved inspector by whom the initial notice was given ; and

(b) to the person shown in the initial notice as the person intending to carry out the work.

(6) A notice under subsection (1), (3) or (5) above shall have the effect of cancelling the initial notice to which it relates with effect from the day on which the notice is given.

Effect of initial notice ceasing to be in force.

45.—(1) The provisions of this section apply where an initial notice ceases to be in force by virtue of paragraph (a) or paragraph (b) of subsection (4) of section 39 above.

(2) Building regulations may provide that, if—

(a) a plans certificate was given before the day on which the initial notice ceased to be in force, and

(b) that certificate was accepted by the local authority (before, on or after that day), and

(c) before that day, that acceptance was not rescinded by a notice under section 42(7) above,

then, with respect to the work specified in the certificate, such of the functions of a local authority referred to in section 40(1) above as may be prescribed for the purposes of this subsection either shall not be exercisable or shall be exercisable only in prescribed circumstances.

(3) If, before the day on which the initial notice ceased to be in force, a final certificate was given in respect of part of the work specified in the initial notice and that certificate was accepted by the local authority (before, on or after that day), the fact that the initial notice has ceased to be in force shall not affect the continuing operation of section 43(3) above in relation to that part of the work.

(4) Notwithstanding anything in subsections (2) and (3) above, for the purpose of enabling the local authority to perform the functions referred to in section 40(1) above in relation to any part of the work not specified in a plans certificate or final certificate, as the case may be, building regulations may require the local authority to be provided with plans which relate not only to that part but also to the part to which the certificate in question relates.

PART II

(5) In any case where this section applies, the reference in subsection (4) of section 65 of the 1936 Act (twelve month time limit for giving certain notices) to the date of the completion of the work in question shall have effect, in relation to a notice under subsection (1) of that section, as if it were a reference to the date on which the initial notice ceased to be in force.

(6) Subject to any provision of building regulations made by virtue of subsection (2) above, if, before the initial notice ceased to be in force, an offence under section 4(6) of the 1961 Act (contravention of provisions of building regulations) was committed with respect to any of the work specified in that notice, summary proceedings for that offence may be commenced by the local authority at any time within six months beginning with the day on which the functions of the local authority referred to in section 40(1) above became exercisable with respect to the provision of building regulations to which the offence relates.

(7) The fact that an initial notice has ceased to be in force shall not affect the right to give a new initial notice relating to any of the work which was specified in the original notice and in respect of which no final certificate has been given and accepted; but where—

(a) a plans certificate has been given in respect of any of that work, and

(b) the conditions in paragraphs (a) to (c) of subsection (2) above are fulfilled with respect to that certificate, and

(c) such a new initial notice is given and accepted,

section 42(1) above shall not apply in relation to so much of the work to which the new initial notice relates as is work specified in the plans certificate.

Supervision of their own work by public bodies

46.—(1) This section applies where a body (corporate or unincorporated) which acts under any enactment for public purposes and not for its own profit and is, or is of a description which is, approved by the Secretary of State in accordance with

Giving, acceptance and effect of public body's notice.

building regulations (in this Part of this Act referred to as a "public body")—

    (a) intends to carry out in relation to a building belonging to it work to which the substantive requirements of building regulations apply; and

    (b) considers that the work can be adequately supervised by its own servants or agents; and

    (c) gives to the local authority in whose district the work is to be carried out notice in the prescribed form (in the enactments relating to building regulations referred to as a "public body's notice") together with such plans of the work as may be prescribed.

(2) A public body's notice shall be of no effect unless it is accepted by the local authority to whom it is given; and that local authority—

    (a) may not reject the notice except on prescribed grounds, and

    (b) shall reject the notice if any of the prescribed grounds exists,

and in any case where the work to which the public body's notice relates is work of such a description that, if plans of it had been deposited with the local authority, the authority could, under any enactment, have imposed requirements as a condition of passing the plans, the local authority may impose the like requirements as a condition of accepting the public body's notice.

(3) Unless, within the prescribed period, the local authority to whom a public body's notice is given give notice of rejection, specifying the ground or grounds in question, the authority shall be conclusively presumed to have accepted the public body's notice and to have done so without imposing any such requirements as are referred to in subsection (2) above.

(4) Section 40 above shall have effect for the purposes of this section—

    (a) with the substitution of a reference to a public body's notice for any reference to an initial notice; and

    (b) with the substitution, in subsection (2)(a), of a reference to subsection (1)(c) of this section for the reference to section 39(1)(b).

(5) The form prescribed for a public body's notice may be such as to require the public body by whom it is to be given—

    (a) to furnish information relevant for the purposes of this Part of this Act, Part II or Part IV of the 1936 Act, Part II of the 1961 Act or any provision of building regulations; and

(b) to enter into undertakings with respect to consultation and other matters.

(6) Where a public body's notice is given and accepted by the local authority to whom it is given, the provisions of Schedule 8 to this Act shall have effect, being provisions which correspond, as near as may be, to those made by the preceding provisions of this Part of this Act for the case where an initial notice is given and accepted.

Supplemental

47.—(1) A person aggrieved by the local authority's rejection of—

(a) an initial notice or a public body's notice, or

(b) a plans certificate, a final certificate, a public body's plans certificate or a public body's final certificate,

may appeal to a magistrates' court acting for the petty sessions area in which is situated land on which will be or has been carried out any work to which the notice or certificate relates.

(2) On an appeal under this section the court shall—

(a) if they determine that the notice or certificate was properly rejected, confirm the rejection; and

(b) in any other case, give a direction to the local authority to accept the notice or certificate.

(3) The procedure on appeal to a magistrates' court under this section shall be by way of complaint for an order and the Magistrates' Courts Act 1980 shall apply to the proceedings. 1980 c. 43.

48.—(1) Every local authority shall keep, in such manner as may be prescribed, a register containing such information as may be prescribed with respect to initial notices, public body's notices and certificates given to them, including information as to whether such notices or certificates have been accepted or rejected.

(2) The information which may be prescribed under subsection (1) above with respect to an initial notice includes information with respect to the insurance cover provided with respect to the work to which the initial notice relates.

(3) The reference in subsection (1) above to certificates is a reference to plans certificates, final certificates, public body's plans certificates, public body's final certificates and certificates given under section 64(2C) of the 1936 Act (which provision is set out in section 56 below).

(4) Every register kept under this section shall be available for inspection by the public at all reasonable hours.

PART II
Offences.

49.—(1) If any person—

(a) gives a notice or certificate which purports to comply with the requirements of this Part of this Act or, as the case may be, of section 64(2C) of the 1936 Act and which contains a statement which he knows to be false or misleading in a material particular, or

(b) recklessly gives a notice or certificate which purports to comply with those requirements and which contains a statement which is false or misleading in a material particular,

he shall be guilty of an offence.

(2) A person guilty of an offence under subsection (1) above shall be liable—

1982 c. 48.

(a) on summary conviction, to a fine not exceeding the statutory maximum (as defined in section 74 of the Criminal Justice Act 1982) or imprisonment for a term not exceeding six months or both; and

(b) on conviction on indictment, to a fine or imprisonment for a term not exceeding two years or both.

(3) Where an approved inspector or person approved for the purposes of section 64(2C) of the 1936 Act is convicted of an offence under this section, the court by or before which he is convicted shall, within one month of the date of conviction, forward a certificate of the conviction to the person by whom the approval was given.

Information, reports and returns.

50. Where an initial notice or a public body's notice has continued in force for any period, the local authority by whom it was accepted may require the approved inspector or public body by whom it was given to furnish them with any information which—

(a) they would have obtained themselves if during that period their function of enforcing building regulations had continued to be exercisable in relation to the work specified in the notice; and

1972 c. 70.

(b) they require for the purpose of performing their duty under section 230 of the Local Government Act 1972 (reports and returns);

and that section shall have effect as if during that period that function had continued to be so exercisable.

Interpretation of Part II.
1936 c. 49.
1961 c. 64.
1974 c. 37.

51.—(1) In this Part of this Act—

" the 1936 Act " means the Public Health Act 1936;

" the 1961 Act " means the Public Health Act 1961;

" the 1974 Act " means the Health and Safety at Work etc. Act 1974;

"approved inspector" has the meaning assigned to it by section 41(1) above;

"contravention", in relation to any provision of building regulations, includes a failure to comply with that provision;

"enactment" includes any enactment contained in a local Act;

"the enactments relating to building regulations" means this Part of this Act and the enactments referred to in section 76(1) of the 1974 Act;

"final certificate" has the meaning assigned to it by section 43(1) above;

"initial notice" has the meaning assigned to it by section 39(1) above;

"plans certificate" has the meaning assigned to it by section 42(1) above;

"public body" and "public body's notice" have the meaning assigned to them by section 46(1) above;

"public body's final certificate" has the meaning assigned to it by paragraph 3 of Schedule 8 to this Act; and

"public body's plans certificate" has the meaning assigned to it by paragraph 2 of that Schedule.

(2) Any reference in this Part of this Act to the carrying out of work includes a reference to the making of a material change of use, as defined by and for the purposes of building regulations.

(3) Any reference in this Part of this Act to an initial notice given by an approved inspector is a reference to a notice given by him jointly with another person as mentioned in section 39(1)(*a*) above.

(4) Sections 74 and 76 of the 1974 Act (construction and interpretation) shall have effect as if the preceding provisions of this Part of this Act (other than subsection (1) above) were included in Part III of the 1974 Act.

PART III

MISCELLANEOUS AMENDMENTS RELATING TO BUILDING WORK

Exemptions and relaxations for public bodies

52.—(1) Building regulations may exempt—

(*a*) a local authority,

(*b*) a county council, and

(*c*) any other body which acts under any enactment for public purposes and not for its own profit and is pre-

Exemption of local authorities etc. from procedural requirements of building regulations.

PART III

scribed for the purpose of this section by building regulations,

from compliance with any requirements of those regulations which are not substantive requirements.

(2) A local authority, county council or other body which is exempted as mentioned in subsection (1) above is in subsection (3) below referred to as an "exempt body".

(3) Without prejudice to the obligation of an exempt body to comply with substantive requirements of building regulations, the function of enforcing building regulations which is conferred on local authorities by section 4(3) of the 1961 Act shall not be exercisable in relation to work carried out by an exempt body and, accordingly—

(a) nothing in subsections (1) to (4) of section 65 of the 1936 Act (powers to require removal or alteration of certain work) shall apply in relation to work so carried out; and

(b) a local authority may not institute proceedings under section 4(6) of the 1961 Act for any contravention of building regulations by an exempt body.

(4) In this section " substantive requirements of building regulations " has the meaning assigned to it by section 76(3) of the 1974 Act.

Power of certain public bodies to relax requirements of building regulations for their own works.

53.—(1) After subsection (2) of section 6 of the 1961 Act there shall be inserted the following subsections:—

" (2A) If—

(a) building regulations so provide as regards any requirement contained in the regulations, and

(b) a public body considers that the operation of any such requirement would be unreasonable in relation to any particular work carried out or proposed to be carried out by or on behalf of the public body,

the public body may give a direction dispensing with or relaxing that requirement.

(2B) In subsection (2A) above " public body " means—

(a) a local authority;

(b) a county council; and

(c) any other body which is prescribed for the purposes of section 52 of the Housing and Building Control Act 1984."

(2) In subsection (1) of section 8 of the 1961 Act (opportunity for representations about proposals to relax building regulations) after the words " local authority ", in the first and second places where they occur, there shall be inserted the words " or other body ", for the words " application is " there shall be substituted the words " direction is proposed to be " and for the words " before publication of the notice " there shall be substituted the words " where the direction is proposed to be made on an application ".

(3) In subsections (2) and (5) of that section after the words " local authority ", in each place where they occur, there shall be inserted the words " or other body " and in subsection (3) of that section for the words " application is " there shall be substituted the words " direction is proposed to be ".

(4) In section 15(1) of the Fire Precautions Act 1971 (consultation with fire authority prior to exercise by local authority of powers under section 6 of the 1961 Act) after the words " local authority ", in the first place where they occur, there shall be inserted the words " or a public body, as defined in section 6(2B) of that Act, proposes to exercise the power conferred on it by section 6(2A) of that Act " and after the words " local authority ", in the second place where they occur, there shall be inserted the words " or other body ".

PART III

1971 c. 40.

Approved documents giving practical guidance

54.—(1) For the purpose of providing practical guidance with respect to the requirements of any provision of building regulations, the Secretary of State or a body designated by him for the purposes of this section may—

(a) approve and issue any document (whether or not prepared by him or by the body concerned), or

(b) approve any document issued or proposed to be issued otherwise than by him or by the body concerned,

if in the opinion of the Secretary of State or, as the case may be, the body concerned the document is suitable for that purpose.

Approval of documents for purposes of building regulations.

(2) References in this section and section 55 below to a document include references to any part of a document; and accordingly, in relation to a document of which part only is approved, any reference in the following provisions of this section or in section 55 below to the approved document is a reference only to the part of it which is approved.

(3) An approval given under subsection (1) above shall take effect in accordance with a notice which is issued by the Secretary of State or, as the case may be, the body giving the approval and which—

(a) identifies the approved document in question;

PART III

(b) states the date on which the approval of it is to take effect; and

(c) specifies the provisions of building regulations for the purposes of which the document is approved.

(4) The Secretary of State or, as the case may be, the body which gave the approval may—

(a) from time to time approve and issue a revision of the whole or any part of an approved document issued by him or it for the purposes of this section; and

(b) approve any revision or proposed revision of the whole or any part of any approved document;

and subsection (3) above shall, with the necessary modifications, apply in relation to an approval which is given under this subsection to a revision as it applies in relation to an approval which is given under subsection (1) above to a document.

(5) The Secretary of State or, as the case may be, the body which gave the approval may withdraw his or its approval of a document under this section; and such a withdrawal of approval shall take effect in accordance with a notice which is issued by the Secretary of State or body concerned and which—

(a) identifies the approved document in question; and

(b) states the date on which the approval of it is to cease to have effect.

(6) References in subsections (4) and (5) above and in section 55 below to an approved document are references to that document as it has effect for the time being, having regard to any revision of the whole or any part of it which has been approved under subsection (4) above.

(7) Where a body ceases to be a body designated by the Secretary of State for the purposes of this section, subsections (4) and (5) above shall have effect as if any approval given by that body had been given by the Secretary of State.

(8) The power to designate a body for the purposes of this section shall be exercisable by order made by statutory instrument which shall be subject to annulment in pursuance of a resolution of either House of Parliament.

Compliance or non-compliance with approved documents.

55.—(1) A failure on the part of any person to comply with an approved document shall not of itself render him liable to any civil or criminal proceedings; but if, in any proceedings whether civil or criminal, it is alleged that any person has at any time contravened a provision of building regulations—

(a) a failure to comply with a document which at that time was approved for the purposes of that provision may be relied upon as tending to establish liability; and

(b) proof of compliance with such a document may be relied on as tending to negative liability.

(2) In any proceedings, whether civil or criminal,—
  (a) a document purporting to be a notice issued as mentioned in section 54(3) above shall be taken to be such a notice unless the contrary is proved; and
  (b) a document which appears to the court to be the approved document to which such a notice refers shall be taken to be that approved document unless the contrary is proved.

Certification and reports

56.—(1) In section 64 of the 1936 Act (passing or rejection of plans etc.) immediately before subsection (3) (appeals to magistrates' courts) there shall be inserted the following subsection—

"(2C) Where the deposited plans are accompanied by—
  (a) a certificate given by a person approved for the purposes of this subsection to the effect that the proposed work, if carried out in accordance with the deposited plans, will comply with such provisions of the regulations prescribed for the purposes of this subsection as may be specified in the certificate, and
  (b) such evidence as may be prescribed that an approved scheme applies, or the prescribed insurance cover has been or will be provided, in relation to the certificate,

the local authority may not except in prescribed circumstances reject the plans on the ground that they are defective with respect to any provisions of the regulations which are so specified or that they show that the proposed work would contravene any of those provisions."

(2) For subsection (3) of section 64 of the 1936 Act there shall be substituted the following subsection—

"(3) In any case where a question arises under this section between a local authority and a person who proposes to carry out any work—
  (a) whether plans of the proposed work are in conformity with building regulations; or
  (b) whether the local authority are prohibited from rejecting plans of the proposed work by virtue of subsection (2C) above,

that person may refer the question to the Secretary of State for his determination; and an application for a reference under this subsection shall be accompanied by such fee as may be prescribed by building regulations."

(3) After that subsection there shall be inserted the following subsection—

"(3A) Where deposited plans accompanied by such a certificate and such evidence as are mentioned in subsection (2C) above are passed by the local authority, or notice of the rejection of deposited plans so accompanied is not given within the prescribed period from the deposit of the plans, the authority may not institute proceedings under section 4(6) of the 1961 Act for any contravention of building regulations which—

(a) arises out of the carrying out of the proposed work in accordance with the plans; and

(b) is a contravention of any of the provisions of the regulations specified in the certificate."

(4) Building regulations may make provision for the approval of persons for the purposes of subsection (2C) of section 64 of the 1936 Act—

(a) by the Secretary of State; or

(b) by a body (corporate or unincorporated) which, in accordance with the regulations, is designated by the Secretary of State for the purpose;

and any such approval may limit the description of work, or the provisions of the regulations, in relation to which the person concerned is so approved.

(5) Any such designation as is referred to in paragraph (b) of subsection (4) above may limit the cases in which and the terms on which the body designated may approve a person and, in particular, may provide that any approval given by the body shall be limited as mentioned in that subsection.

(6) There shall be paid on an application for any such approval as is referred to in subsection (4) above—

(a) where the application is made to the Secretary of State, such fee as may be prescribed by building regulations;

(b) where the application is made to a body designated by him as mentioned in that subsection, such fee as that body may determine.

(7) The Secretary of State may approve for the purposes of subsection (2C) of section 64 of the 1936 Act any scheme which appears to him to secure the provision of adequate insurance cover in relation to any certificate which is given under paragraph (a) of that subsection and is a certificate to which the scheme applies.

(8) Building regulations may prescribe for the purposes of subsection (2C) of section 64 of the 1936 Act the insurance cover which is to be provided in relation to any certificate which

is given under paragraph (*a*) of that subsection and is not a certificate to which an approved scheme applies and may, in particular, prescribe the form and content of policies of insurance.

(9) Building regulations may—
  (*a*) contain provision prescribing the period for which, subject to any provision made by virtue of paragraph (*b*) or (*c*) below, any such approval as is referred to in subsection (4) above shall continue in force;
  (*b*) contain provision precluding the giving of, or requiring the withdrawal of, any such approval as is referred to in that subsection in such circumstances as may be prescribed by the regulations;
  (*c*) contain provision authorising the withdrawal of any such approval or designation as is so referred to;
  (*d*) provide for the maintenance by the Secretary of State of a list of bodies who are for the time being designated by him as mentioned in subsection (4) above and for the maintenance by the Secretary of State and by each designated body of a list of persons for the time being approved by him or them as mentioned in that subsection;
  (*e*) make provision for the supply to local authorities of copies of any list of approved persons maintained by virtue of paragraph (*d*) above and for such copy lists to be made available for inspection; and
  (*f*) make provision for the supply, on payment of a prescribed fee, of a certified copy of any entry in a list maintained by virtue of paragraph (*d*) above or in a copy list held by a local authority by virtue of paragraph (*e*) above.

(10) Unless the contrary is proved, in any proceedings (whether civil or criminal) a document which appears to the court to be a certified copy of an entry either in a list maintained as mentioned in subsection (9)(*d*) above or in a copy of such a list supplied as mentioned in subsection (9)(*e*) above—
  (*a*) shall be presumed to be a true copy of an entry in the current list so maintained; and
  (*b*) shall be evidence of the matters stated therein.

57.—(1) After section 65 of the 1936 Act there shall be inserted the sections set out in Schedule 9 to this Act.

Methods of challenging section 65 notices.

(2) Section 67 of the 1936 Act (joint applications to the Secretary of State for determination of certain questions relating to building regulations) shall cease to have effect except as respects applications referred to the Secretary of State before this subsection comes into force.

PART III

Miscellaneous

Charges by local authorities for performing functions relating to building regulations.

58. Building regulations may authorise local authorities, subject to and in accordance with the regulations, to fix by means of schemes and to recover such charges for or in connection with the performance of functions of theirs relating to building regulations as they may determine in accordance with principles prescribed by the regulations.

Amendments of enactments relating to building regulations.

1974 c. 37.

59.—(1) In section 9(3) of the 1961 Act (consultation with Building Regulations Advisory Committee and other bodies before making building regulations) after the word " regulations ", in the first place where it occurs, there shall be inserted the words " containing substantive requirements as defined in section 76(3) of the Health and Safety at Work etc. Act 1974 ".

(2) The following provisions of the 1974 Act, namely—
   (a) subsection (5) of section 61 (which provides for the repeal of section 71 of the 1936 Act but has not been brought into force) ; and
   (b) subsections (6) and (7) of section 63 (which make provision consequential on that repeal),
shall cease to have effect.

(3) In Schedule 6 to the 1974 Act (amendments of enactments relating to building regulations) paragraphs 1, 2, 5(a), 5(d), 6 and 7 (most of which are not yet in operation and none of which is yet fully in operation) shall be deemed not to have been enacted, and accordingly (and having regard to section 53(1) above)—
   (a) subsection (4) of section 64 of the 1936 Act and section 6 of the 1961 Act shall have effect as set out in Schedule 10 to this Act, and
   (b) section 65 of the 1936 Act and sections 7 and 8 of the 1961 Act shall continue to have effect (for all purposes) without regard to any provision of the said Schedule 6.

Amendments of enactments relating to sanitation and buildings.

60.—(1) Part XII of the 1936 Act (enforcement and other general provisions) shall have effect as if so much of Part II of the 1961 Act (sanitation and buildings) as does not relate to building regulations were contained in Part II of the 1936 Act.

(2) In the following provisions, namely—
   (a) so much of Part II of the 1936 Act (sanitation and buildings) as does not relate to building regulations ;
   (b) sections 137 and 138 of that Act (certain buildings to be supplied with water) ; and
   (c) so much of Part II of the 1961 Act as does not relate to building regulations,
expressions which are defined by subsection (1) of section 82 of the 1974 Act shall have the meanings given by that subsection.

61.—(1) The Building Control Act 1966 (which regulates building and constructional work) shall cease to have effect.

(2) In consequence of subsection (1) above, the enactments mentioned in Part I of Schedule 12 to this Act are hereby repealed to the extent specified in the third column of that Schedule.

PART III

Repeal of the Building Control Act 1966.
1966 c. 27.

62.—(1) In this Part of this Act—

"the 1936 Act" means the Public Health Act 1936;

"the 1961 Act" means the Public Health Act 1961;

"the 1974 Act" means the Health and Safety at Work etc. Act 1974;

"contravention", in relation to any provision of building regulations, includes a failure to comply with that provision;

"local authority" has the meaning assigned to it by subsection (2)(*a*) of section 76 of the 1974 Act.

(2) Any reference in this Part of this Act to the carrying out of work includes a reference to the making of a material change of use, as defined by and for the purposes of building regulations.

Interpretation of Part III.
1936 c. 49.
1961 c. 64.
1974 c. 37.

Part IV

Miscellaneous and General

63.—(1) There shall be paid out of money provided by Parliament the administrative expenses of the Secretary of State under this Act and any increase attributable to this Act in the sums so payable under any other enactment.

(2) There shall be paid out of or into the Consolidated Fund or the National Loans Fund any increase attributable to this Act in the sums so payable under any other enactment.

Financial provisions.

64. The enactments mentioned in Schedule 11 to this Act shall have effect subject to the amendments there specified (being minor amendments and amendments consequential on the preceding provisions of this Act).

Minor and consequential amendments.

65. The enactments mentioned in Part II of Schedule 12 to this Act are hereby repealed to the extent specified in the third column of that Schedule.

Repeals.

C

PART IV
Short title, commencement and extent.

1974 c. 37.

1936 c. 49.

66.—(1) This Act may be cited as the Housing and Building Control Act 1984.

(2) The following provisions of this Act namely—
    (*a*) sections 42(2), 56(2), 57(2) and 58 ;
    (*b*) so far as relating to the amendments of section 69 of the Health and Safety at Work etc. Act 1974, section 64 and Schedule 11 ; and
    (*c*) so far as relating to the repeals of section 67 of the Public Health Act 1936 and section 62(3) of the said Act of 1974, section 65 and Part II of Schedule 12,

shall come into force on such day as the Secretary of State may by order made by statutory instrument appoint ; and different days may be so appointed for different provisions or for different purposes.

(3) Except as provided by subsection (2) above, this Act shall come into force at the end of the period of two months beginning with the day on which this Act is passed.

(4) This Act does not extend to Scotland or Northern Ireland.

SCHEDULES

SCHEDULE 1

Section 1.

EXTENSION OF RIGHT TO BUY TO CERTAIN CASES WHERE LANDLORD
DOES NOT OWN FREEHOLD

1. In section 1(8) (right to acquire freehold or long lease) and section 10(1)(*a*) (notice of purchase price and right to a mortgage) of the 1980 Act for the words " long lease " there shall be substituted the word " lease ".

2. In section 6(4)(*a*) of the 1980 Act (assumptions on the grant of a lease) for the words from " for 125 years " onwards there shall be substituted the words " with vacant possession for the appropriate term defined in sub-paragraph (2) of paragraph 11 of Schedule 2 to this Act (but subject to sub-paragraph (3) of that paragraph) ".

3. In section 14 of the 1980 Act (change of landlord after notice claiming right to buy or right to a mortgage) for the words " the freehold of " there shall be substituted the words " the interest of the landlord in ".

4. In section 16(1) of the 1980 Act (completion) for paragraphs (*a*) and (*b*) there shall be substituted the following paragraphs—

" (*a*) if the dwelling-house is a house and the landlord owns the freehold, a grant of the dwelling-house for an estate in fee simple absolute ; and

(*b*) if the landlord does not own the freehold or (whether or not the landlord owns it) the dwelling-house is a flat, a grant of a lease of the dwelling-house for the appropriate term defined in sub-paragraph (2) of paragraph 11 of Schedule 2 to this Act (but subject to sub-paragraph (3) of that paragraph) ; ".

5. At the end of section 17 of the 1980 Act (conveyance of freehold and grant of lease) there shall be inserted the words " and other matters ".

6. Section 18 of the 1980 Act (right to a mortgage—terms of mortgage deed) shall be renumbered as subsection (1) of that section, in that provision as so renumbered the words from " but the Secretary of State " onwards shall be omitted and after that provision as so renumbered there shall be inserted the following subsections—

" (2) Where the mortgagor's interest in the dwelling-house is leasehold and the term of the lease is less than 25 years, subsection (1)(*b*) above shall have effect as if the reference to 25 years were a reference to the term of the lease.

(3) The Secretary of State may by order prescribe additional terms to be contained in any deed by which a mortgage is effected in pursuance of this Chapter or vary the provisions of subsections (1)(*a*) and (*b*) and (2) above, but only in relation to deeds executed after the order comes into force."

SCH. 1

1925 c. 21.

7. In subsection (3) of section 20 of the 1980 Act (registration of title) for the words " subsection (2) " there shall be substituted the words " subsection (1)(*b*) " and for subsections (1) and (2) of that section there shall be substituted the following subsections—

" (1) Where the landlord's title to the dwelling-house is not registered—

(*a*) section 123 of the Land Registration Act 1925 (compulsory registration of title) shall apply in relation to the conveyance of the freehold or the grant of a lease in pursuance of this Chapter whether or not the dwelling-house is in an area in which an Order in Council under section 120 of that Act is for the time being in force and, in the case of a lease, whether or not the lease is granted for a term of not less than 40 years;

(*b*) the landlord shall give the tenant a certificate stating that the landlord is entitled to convey the freehold or make the grant subject only to such incumbrances, rights and interests as are stated in the conveyance or grant or summarised in the certificate; and

(*c*) section 8 of that Act (application for registration of leasehold land) shall apply in relation to a lease granted in pursuance of this Chapter notwithstanding that it is a lease for a term of which not more than 21 years are unexpired.

(1A) Where the landlord's interest in the dwelling-house is a lease, a certificate under subsection (1)(*b*) above shall also state particulars of that lease and, with respect to each superior title, the following particulars, namely—

(*a*) where it is registered, the title number;

(*b*) where it is not registered, whether it was investigated in the usual way on the grant of the landlord's lease.

(2) Where the landlord's title to the dwelling-house is registered, section 22 of the said Act of 1925 (registration of dispositions of leaseholds) shall apply in relation to a lease granted in pursuance of this Chapter notwithstanding that it is granted for a term not exceeding 21 years."

8. In section 24 of the 1980 Act (vesting orders)—

(*a*) in subsection (3) after the word " If " there shall be inserted the words " the landlord's title to " and the word " land " shall be omitted;

(*b*) in subsection (4) after the words " an absolute title " there shall be inserted the words " or, as the case may require, a good leasehold title "; and

(*c*) in subsection (5) after the word " Where " there shall be inserted the words " the landlord's title to " and the word " land " shall be omitted.

9. After paragraph 5 of Part I of Schedule 1 to the 1980 Act (circumstances in which right to buy does not arise) there shall be inserted the following paragraph—

Sch. 1

" 6.—(1) The dwelling-house is held by the landlord on a tenancy from the Crown.

(2) This paragraph does not apply if either—
   (a) the landlord is entitled to grant a lease in pursuance of this Chapter without the concurrence of the appropriate authority (disregarding for this purpose paragraph 19A of Schedule 2 to this Act) ; or
   (b) the appropriate authority notifies the landlord that as regards any Crown interest affected the authority will give its consent to the granting of such a lease.

(3) For the purposes of this paragraph 'tenancy from the Crown' means a tenancy of land in which there is a Crown interest superior to the tenancy and 'Crown interest' and 'appropriate authority' in relation to a Crown interest mean respectively—
   (a) an interest comprised in the Crown Estate, and the Crown Estate Commissioners or other government department having the management of the land in question ;
   (b) an interest belonging to Her Majesty in right of the Duchy of Lancaster, and the Chancellor of the Duchy ;
   (c) an interest belonging to the Duchy of Cornwall, and such person as the Duke of Cornwall or the possessor for the time being of the Duchy appoints ;
   (d) any other interest belonging to a government department or held on behalf of Her Majesty for the purposes of a government department, and that department."

10.—(1) For paragraph 11 of Schedule 2 to the 1980 Act (terms of leases) there shall be substituted—

" 11.—(1) A lease shall be for the appropriate term defined in sub-paragraph (2) below (but subject to sub-paragraph (3) below) and at a rent not exceeding £10 per annum, and the following provisions shall have effect with respect to the other terms of the lease.

(2) If at the time the grant is made the landlord's interest in the dwelling-house is not less than a lease for a term of which more than 125 years and five days are then unexpired the appropriate term is a term of not less than 125 years ; in any other case it is a term expiring five days before the term of the landlord's lease of the dwelling-house (or, as the case may require, five days before the first date on which the term of any lease under which the landlord holds any part of the dwelling-house is to expire).

(3) If the dwelling-house is a flat contained in a building which also contains one or more other flats and the landlord has, since

the passing of this Act, granted a lease of one or more of them for the appropriate term, the lease of the dwelling-house may be for a term expiring at the end of the term for which the other lease (or one of the other leases) was granted."

(2) In paragraph 12 (common use of premises and facilities) after the word " Where " there shall be inserted the words " the dwelling-house is a flat and ".

(3) In paragraph 13 of that Schedule (covenants by landlord)—

(a) sub-paragraph (1) shall be renumbered as sub-paragraph (1A) of that paragraph;

(b) at the beginning of that provision as so renumbered there shall be inserted the words " Subject to paragraph 13A(3) below ";

(c) immediately before that provision as so renumbered there shall be inserted the following sub-paragraph—

" (1) This paragraph applies where the dwelling-house is a flat."; and

(d) in sub-paragraph (2) for the words " sub-paragraph (1)(a) " there shall be substituted the words " sub-paragraph (1A)(a) ".

(4) After paragraph 13 of that Schedule there shall be inserted the following paragraph—

" 13A.—(1) This paragraph applies where the landlord's interest in the dwelling-house is leasehold.

(2) There shall be implied, by virtue of this Schedule, a covenant by the landlord to pay the rent reserved by the landlord's lease and, except in so far as they fall to be discharged by the tenant, to discharge its obligations under the covenants contained in that lease.

(3) A covenant implied by virtue of paragraph 13(1A) above shall not impose on the landlord any obligations which the landlord is not entitled to discharge under the provisions of the landlord's lease or a superior lease.

(4) Where the landlord's lease or a superior lease or any agreement collateral to the landlord's lease or a superior lease contains a covenant by any person imposing obligations which, but for sub-paragraph (3) above, would be imposed by a covenant implied by virtue of paragraph 13(1A) above, there shall be implied by virtue of this Schedule, a covenant by the landlord to use its best endeavours to secure that that person's obligations under the first mentioned covenant are discharged."

(5) In paragraph 14 of that Schedule (covenant by tenant) for the words from " to keep " onwards there shall be substituted the following paragraphs—

" (a) where the dwelling-house is a house, to keep the dwelling-house in good repair (including decorative repair);

(b) where the dwelling-house is a flat, to keep the interior of the dwelling-house in such repair."

SCH. 1

(6) Paragraph 15 of that Schedule (avoidance of certain agreements) shall be renumbered as sub-paragraph (1) of that paragraph, in that provision as so renumbered paragraph (*b*) and the words " and paragraph 16 below " shall be omitted and after that provision as so renumbered there shall be inserted the following sub-paragraph—

" (2) Where the dwelling-house is a flat, any provision of the lease or of any agreement collateral to it shall be void in so far as it purports—

(*a*) to enable the landlord to recover from the tenant any part of any costs incurred by the landlord in discharging or insuring against any obligations imposed by a covenant implied by virtue of paragraph 13(1A)(*a*) or (*b*) above ; or

(*b*) to enable any person to recover from the tenant any part of any costs incurred, whether by him or by any other person, in discharging or insuring against any obligations to the like effect as obligations which, but for paragraph 13A(3) above, would be imposed by a covenant so implied ;

but subject to paragraph 16 below."

11.—(1) For the heading of Part IV of Schedule 2 to the 1980 Act (charges on freehold) there shall be substituted the heading " CHARGES AND OTHER MATTERS ".

(2) In paragraph 18 of that Schedule for the words " the freehold ", where first occurring, there shall be substituted the words " the interest of the landlord ".

(3) After paragraph 19 of that Schedule there shall be inserted the following paragraph—

" 19A. Any provision of a lease held by the landlord or a superior landlord, or of any agreement (whenever made) shall be void in so far as it would otherwise—

(*a*) prohibit or restrict the grant of a lease in pursuance of the right to buy or the subsequent disposal (whether by way of assignment, sub-lease or otherwise) of a lease so granted ; or

(*b*) authorise any forfeiture or impose on the landlord or superior landlord any penalty or disability in the event of a lease being granted in pursuance of the right to buy or of a subsequent disposal of a lease so granted."

12. After sub-paragraph (2) of paragraph 1 of Schedule 3 to the 1980 Act (tenancies which are not secure tenancies) there shall be inserted the following sub-paragraph—

" (2A) For the purposes of this paragraph a tenancy granted in pursuance of Chapter I of Part I of this Act is a long tenancy notwithstanding that it is granted for a term not exceeding 21 years."

Section 3.

SCHEDULE 2

SCHEDULE INSERTED AFTER SCHEDULE 1 TO 1980 ACT

SCHEDULE 1A

QUALIFICATION AND DISCOUNT

PART I

DETERMINATION OF RELEVANT PERIOD FOR THE PURPOSES OF SECTIONS 1(3) AND 7(1)

1. The period to be taken into account for the purposes of section 1(3) of this Act and the period which under section 7(1) of this Act is to be taken into account for the purposes of discount shall be the period qualifying, or the aggregate of the periods qualifying, under the following provisions of this Part of this Schedule.

2.—(1) A period qualifies under this paragraph if it is a period during which, before the relevant time—
   (a) the secure tenant;
   (b) the secure tenant's spouse; or
   (c) the secure tenant's deceased spouse,

was a public sector tenant or the spouse of a public sector tenant.

(2) A period shall not qualify by virtue of sub-paragraph (1)(a), (b) or (c) above as a period during which the person there mentioned was the spouse of a public sector tenant unless during that period that person occupied as his only or principal home the dwelling-house of which his spouse was such a tenant.

(3) A period shall not qualify by virtue of sub-paragraph (1)(b) above unless the secure tenant and his spouse were living together at the relevant time.

(4) A period shall not qualify by virtue of sub-paragraph (1)(c) above unless the secure tenant and his deceased spouse were living together at the time of the death.

(5) For the purposes of this paragraph a person who, as a joint tenant under a public sector tenancy, occupied a dwelling-house as his only or principal home shall be treated as the public sector tenant under that tenancy.

3.—(1) A period qualifies under this paragraph if it is a period during which, before the relevant time—
   (a) the secure tenant;
   (b) the secure tenant's spouse; or
   (c) the secure tenant's deceased spouse,

was an armed forces occupier or the spouse of an armed forces occupier.

(2) A period shall not qualify by virtue of sub-paragraph (1)(a), (b) or (c) above as a period during which the person there mentioned was the spouse of an armed forces occupier unless during that period that person occupied the accommodation of which his spouse was such an occupier.

SCH. 2

(3) A period shall not qualify by virtue of sub-paragraph (1)(*b*) above unless the secure tenant and his spouse were living together at the relevant time.

(4) A period shall not qualify by virtue of sub-paragraph (1)(*c*) above unless the secure tenant and his deceased spouse were living together at the time of the death.

4.—(1) This paragraph applies where the public sector tenant of a dwelling-house died or otherwise ceased to be a public sector tenant of the dwelling-house, and thereupon a child of his who occupied the dwelling-house as his only or principal home (in this paragraph referred to as " the new tenant ") became the public sector tenant of the dwelling-house (whether under the same or under another public sector tenancy).

(2) A period during which the new tenant, since reaching the age of sixteen, occupied as his only or principal home a dwelling-house of which a parent of his was the public sector tenant or one of joint tenants under a public sector tenancy, being either—
  (*a*) the period at the end of which he became the public sector tenant ; or
  (*b*) a period ending not earlier than two years before another period falling within this sub-paragraph,
shall be regarded for the purposes of paragraph 2 above as a period during which he was a public sector tenant.

(3) For the purposes of this paragraph two persons shall be treated as parent and child if they would be so treated under paragraphs (*a*) and (*b*) of section 50(3) of this Act.

PART II

REDUCTION OF DISCOUNT IN CERTAIN CIRCUMSTANCES

5. There shall be deducted from the discount an amount equal to any previous discount qualifying, or the aggregate of any previous discounts qualifying, under paragraph 6 below.

6.—(1) A previous discount qualifies under this paragraph if it was given—
  (*a*) to the person or one of the persons exercising the right to buy ;
  (*b*) to the spouse of that person or one of those persons ; or
  (*c*) to the deceased spouse of that person or one of those persons.

(2) A previous discount shall not qualify by virtue of sub-paragraph (1)(*b*) above unless the person concerned and his spouse were living together at the relevant time.

(3) A previous discount shall not qualify by virtue of sub-paragraph (1)(*c*) above unless the person concerned and his deceased spouse were living together at the time of the death.

SCH. 2

7.—(1) Where the whole or any part of a previous discount has been recovered by the person by whom it was given (whether by the receipt of a payment determined by reference to the discount or by a reduction so determined of any consideration given by that person or in any other way), so much of the discount as has been so recovered shall be disregarded for the purposes of paragraph 6 above.

(2) Any reference in this paragraph to the person by whom a previous discount was given includes a reference to any successor in title of his.

8. Where a previous discount was given to two or more persons jointly, paragraphs 6 and 7 above shall be construed as if each of those persons had been given an equal proportion of that discount.

PART III

SUPPLEMENTAL

9.—(1) For the purposes of this Schedule, a tenancy which is not a long tenancy and under which a dwelling-house is let as a separate dwelling is a public sector tenancy at any time when the conditions described below as the landlord condition and the tenant condition are satisfied.

(2) The landlord condition is that the interest of the landlord belongs to—

(a) a local authority within the meaning of section 50(1) of this Act, a county council, a district council within the meaning of the Local Government Act (Northern Ireland) 1972 or, in Scotland, a regional, district or islands council, a joint board or joint committee of such a council or the common good of such a council or any trust under its control ; [1972 c. 9 (N.I.).]

(b) the Housing Corporation ;

(c) the Scottish Special Housing Association ;

(d) the Northern Ireland Housing Executive ;

(e) a development corporation established by an order made or having effect as if made under the New Towns Act 1981 or the New Towns (Scotland) Act 1968 or an urban development corporation within the meaning of Part XVI of the Local Government Planning and Land Act 1980 ; [1981 c. 64. 1968 c. 16. 1980 c. 65.]

(f) the Commission for the New Towns ;

(g) the Development Board for Rural Wales ;

(h) a housing association which falls within paragraph (a) of subsection (3) of section 15 of the 1977 Act but does not fall within paragraph (d) of that subsection ;

(i) a housing association which falls within paragraph (e) of section 10(2) of the Tenants' Rights, Etc. (Scotland) Act 1980 but is not a registered society within the meaning of section 11 of that Act ; [1980 c. 52.]

(j) a registered housing association within the meaning of Chapter II of Part II of the Housing (Northern Ireland) Order 1983 ; [S.I. 1983/1118 (N.I. 15).]

(*k*) a housing co-operative within the meaning of Schedule 20 to this Act or section 5 of the Housing Rents and Subsidies (Scotland) Act 1975 ; or

(*l*) any predecessor of any person falling within the foregoing paragraphs ;

or that, in such circumstances as may be prescribed for the purposes of this sub-paragraph by order of the Secretary of State, the interest of the landlord belongs to a person who is so prescribed.

(3) The tenant condition is that the tenant is an individual and occupies the dwelling-house as his only or principal home or, where the tenancy is a joint tenancy, each of the joint tenants is an individual and at least one of them occupies the dwelling-house as his only or principal home.

(4) References in this paragraph to a public sector tenancy or a public sector tenant are, in relation to any time before the commencement of Part I of the 1984 Act, references to a tenancy which would have been a public sector tenancy if that Part had then been in force or to a person who would have then been a public sector tenant ; and for the purpose of determining whether a person would have been a public sector tenant and his tenancy a public sector tenancy, a housing association shall be deemed to have been registered under Part II of the 1974 Act, or Chapter II of Part VII of the Housing (Northern Ireland) Order 1981, if it is or was so registered at any later time.

(5) Where a person who is not the tenant of a dwelling-house has a licence (whether or not granted for a consideration) to occupy the dwelling-house and the circumstances are such that, if the licence were a tenancy, it would be a public sector tenancy, then, subject to sub-paragraph (6) below, this Schedule applies to the licence as it applies to a public sector tenancy and, as so applying, has effect as if expressions appropriate to a licence were substituted for " landlord ", " tenant ", " public sector tenant ", " tenancy " and " public sector tenancy ".

(6) Sub-paragraph (5) above does not apply to a licence which was granted as a temporary expedient to a person who entered a dwelling-house or any other land as a trespasser (whether or not before another licence to occupy that or another dwelling-house had been granted to him).

10.—(1) In this Schedule—

" armed forces occupier " means a person who occupies accommodation provided for him as a member of the regular armed forces of the Crown ;

" conveyance " means a conveyance of the freehold or an assignment of a long lease ;

" dwelling-house " includes a house within the meaning of the 1957 Act ;

" grant " means a grant of a long lease ;

" long lease " means a lease creating a long tenancy within the meaning of paragraph 1 of Schedule 3 to this Act or a tenancy falling within paragraph 1 of Schedule 2 to the Housing (Northern Ireland) Order 1983 ;

SCH. 2

"previous discount" means a discount which was given, before the relevant time, on a conveyance or grant with respect to which the requirements of sub-paragraph (2) below were satisfied;

"public sector tenant" means a tenant under a public sector tenancy;

1975 c. 24.

"regular armed forces of the Crown" has the same meaning as in section 1 of the House of Commons Disqualification Act 1975;

"relevant time" has the meaning given by section 3(5) of this Act.

(2) The requirements of this sub-paragraph are satisfied with respect to a conveyance or grant of a dwelling-house if the vendor or lessor is—

(*a*) a person falling within paragraph 9(2) above; or

(*b*) in such circumstances as may be prescribed for the purposes of this sub-paragraph by order of the Secretary of State, a person who is so prescribed.

Section 12.

SCHEDULE 3

TERMS OF A SHARED OWNERSHIP LEASE

Tenant's initial share

1.—(1) Subject to sub-paragraph (2) below, the tenant's initial share in the dwelling-house shall be as stated in his notice under section 13(1) of this Act.

(2) The tenant's initial share in the dwelling-house shall be a multiple of the prescribed percentage and shall not be less than the minimum initial share.

(3) The lease shall state the tenant's initial share in the dwelling-house.

(4) In this paragraph "minimum initial share" means 50 per cent. or such other percentage as the Secretary of State may by order prescribe.

(5) In this paragraph and paragraph 3 below "the prescribed percentage" means 12.5 per cent. or such other percentage as the Secretary of State may by order prescribe.

Tenant's initial contribution

2.—(1) The consideration for the grant of the lease (in this Part of this Act referred to as the tenant's initial contribution) shall be determined by the formula—

$$C = \frac{S(V - D)}{100}$$

where—

$C =$ the tenant's initial contribution;

$S =$ the tenant's initial share expressed as a percentage;

$V =$ the amount agreed between the parties or determined

by the district valuer as the amount which, under this paragraph, is to be taken as the value of the dwelling-house at the relevant time;

D = the discount which, if the tenant were exercising the right to buy, would be applicable under section 7 of the 1980 Act.

(2) The value of the dwelling-house at the relevant time shall be taken to be the price which, at that time, it would realise if sold on the open market by a willing vendor—

(a) where the dwelling-house is a house and the landlord owns the freehold, on the assumptions stated in subsection (3) of section 6 of the 1980 Act;

(b) where the landlord does not own the freehold or (whether or not the landlord owns it) the dwelling-house is a flat, on the assumptions stated in subsection (4) of that section,

and (in either case) disregarding any improvements made by any of the persons specified in subsection (5) of that section and any failure by any of those persons to keep the dwelling-house in good internal repair.

Additional shares

3.—(1) The lease shall contain provision enabling the tenant to acquire additional shares in the dwelling-house; and the right so conferred shall be exercisable at any time during the term of the lease on the tenant serving written notice on the landlord.

(2) Subject to sub-paragraph (3) below, an additional share shall be as stated in the tenant's notice under sub-paragraph (1) above.

(3) An additional share shall be the prescribed percentage or a multiple of the prescribed percentage.

(4) Where the tenant claims to exercise the right to acquire an additional share, the landlord shall, as soon as practicable, serve on the tenant a written notice stating—

(a) the amount which, in the opinion of the landlord, should be the amount of the consideration for that share determined in accordance with paragraph 4(1) below on the assumption that the share is as stated in the notice under sub-paragraph (1) above; and

(b) the effective discount on an acquisition of that share for that consideration determined in accordance with paragraph 6(3) below.

(5) Where the dwelling-house is a house and the landlord owns the freehold, the lease shall also provide that, on his acquiring an additional share such that his total share will be 100 per cent., the tenant shall be entitled to require the freehold to be conveyed either to himself or to such other person as he may direct; and the right so conferred shall be exercisable at any time during the term of the lease on the tenant serving written notice on the landlord.

(6) As soon as practicable after such a right as is mentioned in sub-paragraph (5) above has become exercisable, the landlord shall serve on the tenant a written notice—

(a) informing the tenant of the right; and

SCH. 3

(b) stating the provisions which, in the opinion of the landlord, should be contained in the conveyance.

(7) A conveyance executed in pursuance of such a right as is mentioned in sub-paragraph (5) above—

(a) shall conform with Parts I and II of Schedule 2 to the 1980 Act (terms of conveyance);

(b) shall preserve the effect of the covenant required by paragraph 6(1) below; and

(c) where the lease contains any such covenant as is mentioned in section 19(1) of the 1980 Act, shall preserve the effect of that covenant.

(8) A notice required by this paragraph may be withdrawn at any time by notice in writing served on the landlord.

(9) Any reference in this Part of this Act to a tenant's total share is a reference to his initial share plus any additional share or shares in the dwelling-house acquired by him.

Additional contributions

4.—(1) The consideration for an additional share (in this Part of this Act referred to as an additional contribution) shall be determined by the formula—

$$C = \frac{S(V - D)}{100}$$

where—

C = the additional contribution;

S = the additional share expressed as a percentage;

V = the amount agreed between the parties or determined by the district valuer as the amount which, under this paragraph, is to be taken as the value of the dwelling-house at the time when the notice under paragraph 3(1) above is served;

D = the discount which, on the assumptions stated in sub-paragraph (2) below, would be applicable under section 7 of the 1980 Act.

(2) The said assumptions are that—

(a) the shared ownership lease had not been granted and the secure tenancy had not come to an end; and

(b) the tenant was exercising the right to buy and his notice under paragraph 3(1) above were a notice under section 5(1) of the 1980 Act.

(3) The value of the dwelling-house at the time when the notice under paragraph 3(1) above is served shall be taken to be the price which, at that time, the interest of the tenant would realise if sold on the open market by a willing vendor on the assumption that any mortgages of that interest and any liability under the covenants required by paragraphs 6(1) and 7(1) below would be discharged by the vendor and disregarding—

(a) any interests in or rights over the dwelling-house created by the tenant;

(b) any improvements made by the tenant or any of the other persons specified in section 6(5) of the 1980 Act; and

(c) any failure by the tenant or any of those persons—

(i) where the dwelling-house is a house, to keep the dwelling-house in good repair (including decorative repair);

(ii) where the dwelling-house is a flat, to keep the interior of the dwelling-house in such repair.

Rent

5.—(1) The lease shall provide that, for any period for which the tenant's total share is less than 100 per cent., the rent payable under the lease shall be determined by the formula—

$$R = \frac{F(100-S)}{100}$$

where—

R = the rent payable;

F = the amount determined by the landlord as the rent which would be payable for that period if the shared ownership lease had not been granted and the secure tenancy had not come to an end, but excluding any element attributable to rates or to services provided by the landlord;

S = the tenant's total share expressed as a percentage.

(2) The lease shall also provide that, for any such period, if the Secretary of State by order so provides—

(a) the rent payable under the lease as so determined; or

(b) any amount payable by the tenant under the lease which is payable, directly or indirectly, for repairs, maintenance or insurance,

shall be adjusted in such manner as may be provided by the order.

(3) The lease shall provide that, for any period for which the tenant's total share is 100 per cent., the rent payable under the lease shall be £10 per annum.

(4) In making a determination under sub-paragraph (1) above, the landlord shall take into account all matters which appear to it to be relevant including, in particular, where comparable dwelling-houses in the locality are let on secure tenancies, the rents payable under those tenancies.

(5) The Secretary of State may by order under sub-paragraph (2) above provide for such adjustment as he considers appropriate having regard to the differing responsibilities for repairs, maintenance and insurance of a tenant under a shared ownership lease and a secure tenant.

(6) In this paragraph "rates" includes charges for services performed, facilities provided or rights made available by a water authority.

SCH. 3

Repayment of discount on early disposal

6.—(1) The lease shall contain a covenant binding on the tenant and his successors in title to pay to the landlord on demand the amount specified in sub-paragraph (2) below if, within a period of five years commencing with the acquisition by the tenant of his initial share or the acquisition by him of an additional share, there is a relevant disposal which is not exempted by sub-paragraph (5) below; but if there is more than one such disposal, then only on the first of them.

(2) The amount payable under the covenant is the aggregate of the following amounts, namely—

(*a*) an amount equal to the effective discount (if any) to which the tenant was entitled on the acquisition of his initial share; and

(*b*) for each additional share acquired by the tenant, an amount equal to the effective discount (if any) to which the tenant was entitled on the acquisition of that share,

but reduced, in each case, by 20 per cent. of the discount for each complete year that elapses after the acquisition and before the disposal.

(3) The effective discount to which the tenant was entitled on the acquisition of his initial share or an additional share shall be determined by the formula—

$$E = \frac{S \times D}{100}$$

where—

E = the effective discount;

S = the tenant's initial share or, as the case may be, the additional share expressed (in either case) as a percentage;

D = the discount which was applicable by virtue of paragraph 2(1) or, as the case may be, paragraph 4(1) above.

(4) A disposal is a relevant disposal for the purposes of this paragraph and paragraphs 7 to 9 below if it is—

(*a*) an assignment of the lease; or

(*b*) the grant of a lease or sub-lease for a term of more than twenty-one years otherwise than at a rack rent,

whether the disposal is of the whole or part of the dwelling-house; and for the purposes of paragraph (*b*) above it shall be assumed that any option to renew or extend a lease or sub-lease, whether or not forming part of a series of options, is exercised, and that any option to terminate a lease or sub-lease is not exercised.

(5) A relevant disposal is exempted by this sub-paragraph if—

(*a*) it is a disposal of the whole of the dwelling-house and an assignment of the lease and the person or each of the persons to whom it is made is a qualifying person;

(*b*) it is a vesting of the whole of the dwelling-house in a person taking under a will or on an intestacy;

(*c*) it is a disposal of the whole of the dwelling-house in pursuance of an order under section 24 of the Matrimonial

1973 c. 18.

Causes Act 1973 or section 2 of the Inheritance (Provision for Family and Dependants) Act 1975 ;

SCH. 3
1975 c. 63.

(d) the property disposed of is acquired compulsorily or by a person who has made or would have made, or for whom another person has made or would have made, a compulsory purchase order authorising its compulsory purchase for the purposes for which it is acquired ; or

(e) the property disposed of is land included in the dwellinghouse by virtue of section 3(4) or 50(2) of the 1980 Act.

(6) For the purposes of sub-paragraph (5)(a) above a person is a qualifying person in relation to a disposal if he—
  (a) is the person or one of the persons by whom it is made ;
  (b) is the spouse or a former spouse of that person or one of those persons ; or
  (c) is a member of the family of that person or one of those persons and has resided with him throughout the period of twelve months ending with the disposal.

(7) Where there is a relevant disposal which is exempted by sub-paragraph (5)(d) or (e) above—
  (a) the covenant required by sub-paragraph (1) above shall not be binding on the person to whom the disposal is made or any successor in title of his ; and
  (b) that covenant and the charge taking effect by virtue of sub-paragraph (10) below shall cease to apply in relation to the property disposed of.

(8) The reference in sub-paragraph (4) above to a lease or sub-lease does not include a mortgage term.

(9) For the purposes of this paragraph and paragraphs 7 to 9 below the grant of an option enabling a person to call for a relevant disposal which is not exempted by sub-paragraph (5) above shall be treated as such a disposal.

(10) Subsections (4) to (6) of section 8 of the 1980 Act shall apply in relation to the liability that may arise under the covenant required by sub-paragraph (1) above and that required by paragraph 7(1) below as they apply in relation to the liability that may arise under the covenant required by subsection (1) of that section.

Payment for outstanding share on disposal

7.—(1) The lease shall contain a covenant binding on the tenant and his successors in title to pay to the landlord on demand for the outstanding share an amount determined in accordance with sub-paragraph (2) below if, at a time when the tenant's total share is less than 100 per cent., there is—
  (a) a relevant disposal which is not exempted by sub-paragraph (5) of paragraph 6 above ; or
  (b) a relevant disposal which is exempted by sub-paragraph (5)(d) of that paragraph (in this paragraph and paragraph 8 below referred to as a " compulsory disposal ").

(2) The amount payable under the covenant shall be determined by the formula—

$$P = \frac{V(100 - S)}{100}$$

D

Sch. 3 where—

P = the amount payable under the covenant;
V = the amount agreed between the parties or determined by the district valuer as the amount which, under this paragraph, is to be taken to be—
  (a) except in the case of a compulsory disposal of part of the dwelling-house, the value at the time of the disposal of the dwelling-house; or
  (b) in the said excepted case, the value at the time of the disposal of the part of the dwelling-house disposed of;
S = the tenant's total share expressed as a percentage.

(3) The value at the time of the disposal of the dwelling-house or the part of the dwelling-house disposed of shall be taken to be the price which, at that time, the interest of the tenant therein would realise if sold on the open market by a willing vendor on the assumption that any mortgages of that interest and any liability under the covenants required by paragraph 6(1) and sub-paragraph (1) above would be discharged by the vendor and disregarding—
  (a) any interests in or rights over the dwelling-house created by the tenant;
  (b) any improvements made by the tenant or any of the other persons specified in section 6(5) of the 1980 Act; and
  (c) any failure by the tenant or any of those persons—
    (i) where the dwelling-house is a house, to keep the dwelling-house in good repair (including decorative repair);
    (ii) where the dwelling-house is a flat, to keep the interior of the dwelling-house in such repair.

(4) The lease shall also provide that, on the discharge of a liability arising under the covenant required by sub-paragraph (1) above,—
  (a) except in the case of a compulsory disposal of part of the dwelling-house, the rent payable under the lease shall be £10 per annum; and
  (b) in the said excepted case, the rent payable under the lease so far as relating to the part of the dwelling-house disposed of shall be £10 per annum.

(5) Where the dwelling-house is a house and the landlord owns the freehold, the lease shall also provide that on the discharge of a liability arising under the covenant required by sub-paragraph (1) above,—
  (a) except in the case of a compulsory disposal of part of the dwelling-house, any person in whom the tenant's interest in the dwelling-house is vested; or
  (b) in the said excepted case, any person in whom the tenant's interest in the part of the dwelling-house disposed of is vested,
shall be entitled to require the freehold thereof to be conveyed either to himself or to such other person as he may direct; and a

right so conferred on any person shall be exercisable at any time during the term of the lease on that person serving written notice on the landlord.

(6) As soon as practicable after such a right as is mentioned in sub-paragraph (5) above has become exercisable by any person, the landlord shall serve on that person a written notice—
   (a) informing him of the right; and
   (b) stating the provisions which, in the opinion of the landlord, should be contained in the conveyance.

(7) A conveyance executed in pursuance of such a right as is mentioned in sub-paragraph (5) above—
   (a) shall conform with Parts I and II of Schedule 2 to the 1980 Act (terms of conveyance); and
   (b) where the lease contains any such covenant as is mentioned in section 19(1) of the 1980 Act, shall preserve the effect of that covenant.

(8) A notice required by sub-paragraph (5) above may be withdrawn at any time by notice in writing served on the landlord.

No disposals of part while share outstanding

8.—(1) The lease shall contain a covenant binding on the tenant and his successors in title that there will be no relevant disposal of part of the dwelling-house, other than a compulsory disposal, at any time when the tenant's total share is less than 100 per cent.

(2) Any disposal in breach of the covenant required by sub-paragraph (1) above shall be void.

Supplemental

9.—(1) The lease shall provide that, in the event of a relevant disposal which is exempted by sub-paragraph (5)(a), (b) or (c) of paragraph 6 above, references to the tenant in the provisions of the lease required by this Schedule shall include references to the person to whom the disposal is made.

(2) The lease shall also provide that, in the event of a relevant disposal which is exempted by sub-paragraph (5)(d) of that paragraph, being a disposal of part of the dwelling-house, references to the dwelling-house in the provisions of the lease required by this Schedule shall be construed as references to the remaining part of the dwelling-house.

10.—(1) Any power to make an order under this Schedule shall be exercisable by statutory instrument which shall be subject to annulment in pursuance of a resolution of either House of Parliament.

(2) Any order under this Schedule—
   (a) may make different provision with respect to different cases or descriptions of case, including different provision for different areas; and
   (b) may contain such transitional provisions as appear to the Secretary of State to be necessary or expedient.

Section 18.

SCHEDULE 4

SERVICE CHARGES IN RESPECT OF CERTAIN HOUSES

Service charge and relevant costs

1.—(1) In this Schedule " service charge " has the meaning given by section 18(1) of this Act.

(2) For the purposes of this Schedule relevant costs are costs or estimated costs (including overheads) incurred or to be incurred in any period (whether the period for which the service charge is payable or an earlier or later period) by or on behalf of the payee or (in the case of a lease) a superior landlord in connection with the matters for which the service charge is payable.

(3) Other expressions used in this Schedule are to be construed in accordance with paragraphs 11 to 13 below.

Limitation of service charges

2. The extent to which relevant costs are taken into account in determining the amount of a service charge payable for any period shall be limited in accordance with paragraph 3 below, and the amount payable shall be limited accordingly; and where the service charge is payable before the relevant costs are incurred—

    (*a*) no greater amount shall be so payable than is reasonable; and

    (*b*) after the relevant costs have been incurred any necessary adjustment shall be made by repayment, reduction of subsequent charges or otherwise.

3. Costs are to be taken into account only to the extent that they are reasonably incurred, and costs incurred on the provision of services or the carrying out of works only if the services or works are of a reasonable standard.

Information as to relevant costs

4.—(1) If the payer requests the payee in writing to supply him with a written summary of the costs incurred in the relevant period defined in sub-paragraph (4) below which are relevant to the service charges payable or demanded as payable by the payer in that or any other period, the payee shall do so within six months of the end of the period or within one month of the request, whichever is the later.

(2) The summary shall set out those costs in a way showing how they are or will be reflected in demands for service charges, and must be certified by a qualified accountant as in his opinion a fair summary complying with this requirement and as being sufficiently supported by accounts, receipts and other documents which have been produced to him.

(3) Where the payer has obtained such a summary as is referred to in sub-paragraph (1) above (whether in pursuance of this paragraph or otherwise) the payer may, within six months of obtaining it, require the payee in writing to afford him reasonable facilities for inspecting the accounts, receipts and other documents supporting the summary and for taking copies or extracts from them, and the payee shall then make such facilities available to the payer for

a period of two months beginning not later than one month after the request is made. Sch. 4

(4) The relevant period mentioned in sub-paragraph (1) above is—
   (a) if the relevant accounts are made up for periods of twelve months, the last such period ending not later than the date of the request; and
   (b) if none are made up for such a period, the period of twelve months ending with the request.

Information held by superior landlord

5.—(1) If a request made under paragraph 4(1) above relates in whole or in part to relevant costs incurred by or on behalf of a superior landlord, and the payee is not in possession of the relevant information—
   (a) he shall in turn make a written request for the relevant information to the person who is his landlord (and so on if that person is not himself the superior landlord) and the superior landlord shall then comply with the request within a reasonable time; and
   (b) it shall be the duty of the payee to comply with the payer's request, or that part of it which relates to the relevant costs incurred by or on behalf of the superior landlord, within the time allowed by paragraph 4 above or within such further time, if any, as is reasonable in the circumstances.

(2) If a request made under paragraph 4(3) above relates to a summary of costs incurred by or on behalf of a superior landlord, the payee shall forthwith inform the payer of that fact and the name and address of the superior landlord, and paragraph 4(3) above shall then apply as if the superior landlord were the payee.

Service of requests under paragraph 4

6. A request under paragraph 4 above shall be deemed to be served on the payee if it is served on a person who receives the service charge on behalf of the payee; and a person on whom a request is so served shall forward it as soon as possible to the payee.

Effect of disposal

7. A disposal of the dwelling-house by the payer shall not affect the validity of a request made under paragraph 4 above before the disposal, but a person shall not be obliged to provide a summary or make the facilities available more than once for the same dwelling-house and for the same period.

Determination of reasonableness

8. Any agreement made by the payer, other than an arbitration agreement within the meaning of section 32 of the Arbitration Act 1950 c. 27. 1950, shall be void in so far as it purports to provide for a determination in a particular manner or on particular evidence of any question whether any amount payable before costs for services, repair, maintenance, insurance or management are incurred is reasonable, whether such costs were reasonably incurred or whether services or works for which costs were incurred are of a reasonable standard.

SCH. 4

1982 c. 48.

Offences

9.—(1) If any person without reasonable excuse fails to perform any duty imposed on him by this Schedule he shall be guilty of an offence and liable on summary conviction to a fine not exceeding level 4 on the standard scale (as defined in section 75 of the Criminal Justice Act 1982).

(2) Where an offence under this paragraph which has been committed by a body corporate is proved to have been committed with the consent or connivance of, or to be attributable to any neglect on the part of, a director, manager, secretary or other similar officer of the body corporate, or any person who was purporting to act in any such capacity, he, as well as the body corporate, shall be guilty of an offence and be liable to be proceeded against and punished accordingly.

(3) Where the affairs of a body corporate are managed by its members, sub-paragraph (2) shall apply in relation to the acts and defaults of a member in connection with his functions of management as if he were a director of the body corporate.

Exceptions

10.—(1) Where the payee is a body mentioned in sub-paragraph (2) below—
   (a) paragraph 9 above does not apply, and
   (b) the persons who are qualified accountants include a member of the Chartered Institute of Public Finance and Accountancy and paragraph 11(2)(b) below does not apply.

(2) The bodies referred to in sub-paragraph (1) above are—
   (a) a local authority or development corporation (as defined in section 50(1) of the 1980 Act),
   (b) the council of a county,
   (c) the Commission for the New Towns,
   (d) the Development Board for Rural Wales.

Definitions

11.—(1) Subject to sub-paragraph (2) below, a person is a qualified accountant if he is either a member of one of the following bodies—
   (a) the Institute of Chartered Accountants in England and Wales;
   (b) the Institute of Chartered Accountants of Scotland;
   (c) the Association of Certified Accountants;
   (d) The Institute of Chartered Accountants in Ireland;
   (e) any other body of accountants established in the United Kingdom and recognised by the Secretary of State for the purposes of section 161(1)(a) of the Companies Act 1948,

1948 c. 38.

or a person who is for the time being authorised by the Secretary of State under section 161(1)(b) of that Act as being a person with similar qualifications obtained outside the United Kingdom.

(2) None of the following is a qualified accountant—
   (a) a body corporate;
   (b) an officer or employee of the payee or, where the payee is a company, of a company which is the payee's holding

company or subsidiary (within the meaning of section 154 of the Companies Act 1948) or a subsidiary of the payee's holding company; and

SCH. 4
1948 c. 38.

(c) a person who is a partner or employee of any such officer or employee.

(3) A Scottish firm is a qualified accountant, notwithstanding sub-paragraph (2)(a) above, if each of the partners in it is a qualified accountant.

12. " Payee " means the person who is entitled to enforce payment of the service charge.

13. " Payer " means the person liable to pay the service charge.

SCHEDULE 5

Section 19.

VESTING OF MORTGAGED DWELLING-HOUSE IN LOCAL AUTHORITY ETC.

Vesting of dwelling-house with leave of court

1.—(1) In any case where this Schedule applies, the authority may, if the county court gives it leave to do so, by deed vest the dwelling-house in itself—

(a) for such estate and interest in the dwelling-house as is the subject of the mortgage or as it would be authorised to sell or convey on exercising its power of sale; and

(b) freed from all estates, interests and rights to which the mortgage has priority,

but subject to all estates, interests and rights which have priority to the mortgage.

(2) Where application for leave under this paragraph is made to the county court, the court may adjourn the proceedings or postpone the date for the execution of the authority's deed for such period or periods as the court thinks reasonable.

(3) Any such adjournment or postponement may be made subject to such conditions with regard to payment by the mortgagor of any sum secured by the mortgage or the remedy of any default as the court thinks fit; and the court may from time to time vary or revoke any such condition.

Effect of vesting

2.—(1) On the vesting of the dwelling-house the authority's mortgage term or charge by way of legal mortgage, and any subsequent mortgage term or charge, shall merge or be extinguished as respects the dwelling-house.

(2) Where the dwelling-house is registered under the Land Registration Acts 1925 to 1971, the Chief Land Registrar shall, on application being made to him by the authority, register the authority as proprietor of the dwelling-house free from all estates, interests and rights to which its mortgage had priority, and he shall not be concerned to inquire whether any of the requirements of this Schedule were complied with.

SCH. 5

(3) Where the authority conveys the dwelling-house, or part of it, to any person—
  (a) he shall not be concerned to inquire whether any of the provisions of this Schedule were complied with; and
  (b) his title shall not be impeachable on the ground that the dwelling-house was not properly vested in the authority or that those provisions were not complied with.

(4) A dwelling-house vested under this Schedule in a local authority (as defined in section 50 of the 1980 Act) shall be treated as acquired under Part V of the 1957 Act.

Compensation and accounting

3.—(1) Where, under paragraph 1 above, the authority has vested the dwelling-house in itself it shall appropriate a fund equal to the aggregate of—
  (a) the amount agreed between the authority and the mortgagor or determined by the district valuer as being the amount which under sub-paragraph (2) below is to be taken as the value of the dwelling-house at the time of the vesting; and
  (b) interest on that amount for the period beginning with the vesting and ending with the appropriation at the rate or rates prescribed for that period under section 32 of the Land Compensation Act 1961.

1961 c. 33.

(2) The value of the dwelling-house at the time of the vesting shall be taken to be the price which, at that time, the interest vested in the authority would realise if sold on the open market by a willing vendor on the assumption that any prior incumbrances to which the vesting is not made subject would be discharged by the vendor.

(3) The fund shall be applied—
  (a) first, in discharging, or paying sums into court for meeting, any prior incumbrances to which the vesting is not made subject;
  (b) secondly, in recovering the costs, charges and expenses properly incurred by the authority as incidental to the vesting of the dwelling-house;
  (c) thirdly, in recovering the mortgage money, interest, costs, and other money (if any) due under the mortgage; and
  (d) fourthly, in recovering any amount which falls to be paid under the covenant required by section 104B(2) of the 1957 Act, section 8(1) of the 1980 Act or paragraph 6(1) or 7(1) of Schedule 3 to this Act or any provision of the conveyance or grant to the like effect;

and any residue then remaining in the fund shall be paid to the person entitled to the mortgaged dwelling-house, or who would have been entitled to give receipts for the proceeds of sale of the dwelling-house if it had been sold in the exercise of the power of sale.

1925 c. 20.

(4) Section 107(1) of the Law of Property Act 1925 (mortgagee's written receipt sufficient discharge for money arising under power of sale) applies to money payable under this Schedule as it applies to money arising under the power of sale conferred by that Act.

SCHEDULE 6

Section 23.

Amendments of Sections 104B and 104C of 1957 Act

Section 104B

1.—(1) In subsection (2) of section 104B of the 1957 Act (repayment of discount on early disposal) for the words " disposal falling within subsection (4) " there shall be substituted the words " relevant disposal which is not exempted by subsection (4A) ".

(2) For subsection (4) of that section there shall be substituted the following subsections—

" (4) A disposal is a relevant disposal for the purposes of this section if it is—

(a) a conveyance of the freehold or an assignment of the lease ; or

(b) the grant of a lease or sub-lease for a term of more than twenty-one years otherwise than at a rack rent,

whether the disposal is of the whole or part of the house ; and for the purposes of paragraph (b) above it shall be assumed that any option to renew or extend a lease or sub-lease, whether or not forming part of a series of options, is exercised, and that any option to terminate a lease or sub-lease is not exercised.

(4A) A relevant disposal is exempted by this subsection if—

(a) it is a disposal of the whole of the house and a conveyance of the freehold or an assignment of the lease and the person or each of the persons to whom it is made is a qualifying person ;

(b) it is a vesting of the whole of the house in a person taking under a will or on an intestacy ;

(c) it is a disposal of the whole of the house in pursuance of an order under section 24 of the Matrimonial Causes Act 1973 or section 2 of the Inheritance (Provision for Family and Dependants) Act 1975 ; 1973 c. 18. 1975 c. 63.

(d) the property disposed of is acquired compulsorily or by a person who has made or would have made, or for whom another person has made or would have made a compulsory purchase order authorising its compulsory purchase for the purposes for which it is acquired ; or

(e) the property disposed of is land falling within paragraph (a) of the definition of ' house ' in section 189(1) of this Act.

(4B) For the purposes of subsection (4A)(a) above a person is a qualifying person in relation to a disposal if he—

(a) is the person or one of the persons by whom it is made ;

(b) is the spouse or a former spouse of that person or one of those persons ; or

(c) is a member of the family of that person or one of those persons (within the meaning of Chapter II of Part I of the Housing Act 1980) and has resided with him throughout the period of twelve months ending with the disposal. 1980 c. 51.

(4C) Where there is a relevant disposal which is exempted by subsection (4A)(*d*) or (*e*) above—

    (*a*) the covenant required by subsection (2) above shall not be binding on the person to whom the disposal is made or any successor in title of his ; and

    (*b*) that covenant and the charge taking effect by virtue of subsection (5) below shall cease to apply in relation to the property disposed of."

(3) In subsection (5) of that section for the words "specified in" there shall be substituted the words "falling within".

(4) After that subsection there shall be inserted the following subsection—

"(5A) The local authority may at any time by written notice served on a body falling within subsection (6) below postpone the charge taking effect by virtue of subsection (5) above to any legal charge securing any amount advanced or further advanced to the purchaser by that body."

(5) For subsection (6) of that section there shall be substituted the following subsection—

"(6) The bodies referred to in subsections (5)(*b*) and (5A) above are—

    (*a*) any building society ;

    (*b*) any body falling within paragraphs 6 to 9 of the Schedule to the Home Purchase Assistance and Housing Corporation Guarantee Act 1978 ; and

    (*c*) any body specified or of a class or description specified in an order made under section 8(5) of the Housing Act 1980."

(6) In subsection (9) of that section, for the words "disposal falling within subsection (4) above" there shall be substituted the words "relevant disposal which is not exempted by subsection (4A) above".

(7) Where any conveyance, grant or assignment executed under section 104 of the 1957 Act or section 122 of the 1980 Act before the commencement date contains the covenant required by section 104B(2) of the 1957 Act, then, as from that date, that covenant shall have effect with such modifications as may be necessary to bring it into conformity with the amendments made by this paragraph.

Section 104C

2.—(1) In subsection (1) of section 104C of the 1957 Act (houses in National Parks and areas of outstanding natural beauty etc.) for the words "by order of the Secretary of State" there shall be substituted the words "under section 19 of the Housing Act 1980" and for the words "and his successors in title" there shall be substituted the words "(including any successor in title of his and any person deriving title under him or any such successor)".

(2) In subsection (2) of that section for the words "or his successors in title" there shall be substituted the words "or a successor in title

of his" and for the words "disposal falling within subsection (4) below" there shall be substituted the words "relevant disposal which is not exempted by section 104B(4A) of this Act".

(3) Subsection (4) of that section shall be omitted.

(4) For subsection (7) of that section there shall be substituted the following subsections—

"(7) Where there is a relevant disposal which is exempted by section 104B(4A)(*d*) or (*e*) of this Act, the covenant mentioned in subsection (1) above shall cease to apply to the property disposed of.

(7A) In this section 'relevant disposal' has the same meaning as in section 104B of this Act."

(5) In subsection (9) of that section for the words from "means" onwards there shall be substituted the words "has the same meaning as in section 19 of the Housing Act 1980".

(6) In subsection (10) of that section for the words "disposal falling within subsection (4) above" there shall be substituted the words "relevant disposal which is not exempted by section 104B(4A) of this Act".

(7) Where any conveyance, grant or assignment executed under section 104 of the 1957 Act or section 122 of the 1980 Act before the commencement date contains such a covenant as is mentioned in section 104C(1) of the 1957 Act, then, as from that date, that covenant—

(*a*) shall be binding not only on the purchaser and any successor in title of his but also on any person deriving title under him or any such successor; and

(*b*) shall have effect with such modifications as may be necessary to bring it into conformity with the amendments made by this paragraph.

SCHEDULE 7
SCHEDULE INSERTED AFTER SCHEDULE 4 TO 1980 ACT
SCHEDULE 4A
GROUNDS FOR WITHHOLDING CONSENT TO ASSIGNMENT BY WAY OF EXCHANGE

Ground 1

The tenant or the proposed assignee is obliged to give up possession of the dwelling-house of which he is the secure tenant in pursuance of an order of the court, or will be so obliged at a date specified in such an order.

Ground 2

Proceedings have been begun for possession of the dwelling-house of which the tenant or the proposed assignee is the secure tenant on one or more of grounds 1 to 5A as set out in Part I of Schedule 4 to this Act or there has been served on the tenant or the proposed assignee a notice under section 33 of this Act which specifies one or more of those grounds and that notice is still in force.

Ground 3

The accommodation afforded by the dwelling-house is substantially more extensive than is reasonably required by the proposed assignee.

Ground 4

The extent of the accommodation afforded by the dwelling-house is not reasonably suitable to the needs of the proposed assignee and his family.

Ground 5

The dwelling-house either forms part of, or is within the curtilage of, a building to which sub-paragraph (2) of paragraph 1 of Part I of Schedule 1 to this Act applies or is situated in a cemetery and (in either case) the dwelling-house was let to the tenant or to a predecessor in title of his in consequence of the tenant or predecessor being in the employment of the landlord or of a body specified in sub-paragraph (3) of that paragraph.

Ground 6

1960 c. 58.

The landlord is a charity within the meaning of the Charities Act 1960 and the proposed assignee's occupation of the dwelling-house would conflict with the objects of the charity.

Ground 7

The dwelling-house has features which are substantially different from those of ordinary dwelling-houses and which are designed to make it suitable for occupation by a physically disabled person who requires accommodation of the kind provided by the dwelling-house and, if the assignment were made, there would no longer be such a person residing in the dwelling-house.

Ground 8

The landlord is a housing association or housing trust which lets dwelling-houses only for occupation (alone or with others) by persons whose circumstances (other than merely financial circumstances) make it especially difficult for them to satisfy their need for housing and, if the assignment were made, there would no longer be such a person residing in the dwelling-house.

Ground 9

The dwelling-house is one of a group of dwelling-houses which it is the practice of the landlord to let for occupation by persons with special needs and a social service or special facility is provided in close proximity to the group of dwelling-houses in order to assist persons with those special needs and, if the assignment were made, there would no longer be a person with those special needs residing in the dwelling-house.

Section 46.

SCHEDULE 8

PROVISIONS CONSEQUENTIAL UPON PUBLIC BODY'S NOTICE

Duration of notice

1.—(1) A public body's notice shall come into force when it is accepted by the local authority, either by notice given within the prescribed period to the public body by which it was given or by virtue of section 46(3) of this Act and, subject to paragraph 3(3) below, shall continue in force until the occurrence of, or the expiry of a prescribed period of time beginning on the date of, such event as may be prescribed.

(2) Building regulations may empower a local authority to extend (whether before or after its expiry) any such period of time as is referred to in sub-paragraph (1) above.

Public body's plans certificates

2.—(1) Where a public body—
- (a) is satisfied that plans of the work specified in a public body's notice given by it have been inspected by a servant or agent of the body who is competent to assess the plans, and
- (b) in the light of that inspection is satisfied that the plans neither are defective nor show that work carried out in accordance with them would contravene any provision of building regulations, and
- (c) has complied with any prescribed requirements as to consultation or otherwise,

the body may give to the local authority a certificate in the prescribed form (in the enactments relating to building regulations referred to as a " public body's plans certificate ").

(2) Building regulations may authorise the giving of a public body's notice combined with a certificate under sub-paragraph (1) above and may prescribe a single form for such a combined notice and certificate ; and where such a prescribed form is used,—
- (a) any reference in this Schedule or in any other provision of Part II of this Act to a public body's notice or to a public body's plans certificate shall be construed as including a reference to that form ; but
- (b) should the form cease to be in force as a public body's notice by virtue of paragraph 1(1) above, nothing in that paragraph shall affect the continuing validity of the form as a public body's plans certificate.

(3) A public body's plans certificate—
- (a) may relate either to the whole or to part only of the work specified in the public body's notice concerned ; and
- (b) shall not have effect unless it is accepted by the local authority to whom it is given.

(4) A local authority to whom a public body's plans certificate is given—
- (a) may not reject the certificate except on prescribed grounds ; and
- (b) shall reject the certificate if any of the prescribed grounds exists.

(5) Unless, within the prescribed period, the local authority to whom a public body's plans certificate is given give notice of rejection, specifying the ground or grounds in question, to the public body by which the certificate was given, the authority shall be conclusively presumed to have accepted the certificate.

(6) If it appears to a local authority by whom a public body's plans certificate has been accepted that the work to which the certificate relates has not been commenced within the period of three years beginning on the date on which the certificate was accepted, the authority may rescind their acceptance of the certificate by notice, specifying the ground or grounds in question, given to the public body.

Public body's final certificates

3.—(1) Where a public body is satisfied that any work specified in a public body's notice given by it has been completed, the body may give to the local authority such certificate with respect to the completion of the work and compliance with building regulations as may be prescribed (in the enactments relating to building regulations referred to as a " public body's final certificate ").

(2) Sub-paragraphs (3) to (5) of paragraph 2 above shall have effect in relation to a public body's final certificate as if any reference in those sub-paragraphs to a public body's plans certificate were a reference to a public body's final certificate.

(3) Where a public body's final certificate has been given with respect to any of the work specified in a public body's notice and that certificate has been accepted by the local authority concerned, the public body's notice shall cease to apply to that work, but the provisions of section 40(1) of this Act, as applied by section 46(4), shall, by virtue of this sub-paragraph, continue to apply in relation to that work as if the public body's notice continued in force in relation to it.

Effects of public body's notice ceasing to be in force

4.—(1) The provisions of this paragraph apply where a public body's notice ceases to be in force by virtue of paragraph 1(1) above.

(2) Building regulations may provide that, if—
   (a) a public body's plans certificate was given before the day on which the public body's notice ceased to be in force, and
   (b) that certificate was accepted by the local authority (before, on or after that day), and
   (c) before that day, that acceptance was not rescinded by a notice under paragraph 2(6) above,
then, with respect to the work specified in the certificate, such of the functions of a local authority referred to in section 40(1) of this Act as may be prescribed for the purposes of this sub-paragraph either shall not be exercisable or shall be exercisable only in prescribed circumstances.

(3) If, before the day on which the public body's notice ceased to be in force, a public body's final certificate was given in respect of part of the work specified in the notice and that certificate was accepted by the local authority (before, on or after that day), the fact that the public body's notice has ceased to be in force shall not affect the continuing operation of paragraph 3(3) above in relation to that part of the work.

(4) Notwithstanding anything in sub-paragraphs (2) and (3) above, for the purpose of enabling the local authority to perform the functions referred to in section 40(1) of this Act in relation to any part of the work not specified in a public body's plans certificate or final certificate, as the case may be, building regulations may require the local authority to be provided with plans which relate not only to that part but also to the part to which the certificate in question relates.

(5) In any case where this paragraph applies, the reference in subsection (4) of section 65 of the 1936 Act (twelve month time limit for giving certain notices) to the date of the completion of the work in question shall have effect, in relation to a notice under subsection (1) of that section, as if it were a reference to the date on which the public body's notice ceased to be in force.

(6) Subject to any provision of building regulations made by virtue of sub-paragraph (2) above, if, before the public body's notice ceased to be in force, an offence under section 4(6) of the 1961 Act (contravention of provisions of building regulations) was committed with respect to any of the work specified in that notice, summary proceedings for that offence may be commenced by the local authority at any time within six months beginning with the day on which the functions of the local authority referred to in section 40(1) of this Act became exercisable with respect to the provision of building regulations to which the offence relates.

(7) Any reference in the preceding provisions of this paragraph to section 40(1) of this Act is a reference to that section as applied by section 46(4) thereof.

Consultation

5. Building regulations may make provision for requiring, in such circumstances as may be prescribed, a public body which has given a public body's notice to consult any prescribed person before taking any prescribed step in connection with any work specified in the notice.

SCHEDULE 9

Section 57(1).

SECTIONS INSERTED AFTER SECTION 65 OF THE 1936 ACT

Obtaining of report where section 65 notice given.

65A.—(1) In any case where—

(a) a person to whom a section 65 notice has been given gives to the local authority by whom the notice was given notice in writing of his intention to obtain from a suitably qualified person a written report concerning work to which the section 65 notice relates, and

(b) such a report is obtained and submitted to the local authority and, as a result of their consideration of it, the local authority withdraw the section 65 notice,

the local authority may pay to the person to whom the section 65 notice was given such amount as appears to

SCH. 9

them to represent the expenses reasonably incurred by him in consequence of their having given him that notice including, in particular, his expenses in obtaining the report.

(2) Subject to subsection (3) of this section, if a person to whom a section 65 notice has been given gives notice under subsection (1)(a) of this section then, so far as regards the matters to which the section 65 notice relates, the reference to twenty-eight days in section 65(3) of this Act shall be construed as a reference to seventy days.

(3) Notice under subsection (1)(a) of this section shall be given before the expiry of the period of twenty-eight days referred to in subsection (3) of section 65 of this Act or, as the case may be, within such longer period as a court allows under that subsection; and where such a longer period has been so allowed before notice is given under subsection (1)(a) of this section, subsection (2) of this section shall not apply.

(4) In this section and in section 65B of this Act a " section 65 notice " means a notice under subsection (1) or subsection (2) of section 65 of this Act.

Appeals against section 65 notices.

65B.—(1) Any person aggrieved by the giving of a section 65 notice may appeal to a magistrates' court acting for the petty sessions area in which is situated land on which has been carried out any work to which the notice relates.

(2) Subject to subsection (3) below, on an appeal under this section the court shall,—

(a) if they determine that the local authority were entitled to give the notice, confirm the notice; and

(b) in any other case, give the local authority a direction to withdraw the notice.

(3) If, in a case where the appeal is against a notice under subsection (2) of section 65 of this Act, the court is satisfied that—

(a) the local authority were entitled to give the notice, but

(b) in all the circumstances of the case the purpose for which was enacted the section of this Act by virtue of which the notice was given has been substantially achieved,

the court may give a direction under subsection (2)(b) of this section.

(4) An appeal under this section shall be brought—

(a) within twenty-eight days of the giving of the section 65 notice; or

(b) in a case where the person to whom the section 65 notice was given gives notice under subsection (1)(a) of section 65A of this Act, within seventy days of the giving of the section 65 notice.

(5) The procedure on appeal to a magistrates' court under this section shall be by way of complaint for an order and the Magistrates' Courts Act 1980 shall apply to the proceedings.

1980 c. 43.

(6) Where an appeal is brought under this section—

(a) the section 65 notice shall be of no effect pending the final determination or withdrawal of the appeal; and

(b) subsection (3) of section 65 of this Act shall have effect in relation to that notice as if after the words " twenty-eight days " there were inserted the words " (beginning, in a case where an appeal is brought under section 65B of this Act, on the date when the appeal is finally determined or, as the case may be, withdrawn) ".

(7) If, on an appeal under this section, there is produced to the court a report which has been submitted to the local authority under subsection (1) of section 65A of this Act, the court, in making any order as to costs, may treat the expenses incurred in obtaining the report as expenses incurred for the purposes of the appeal.

SCHEDULE 10

Section 59(3).

SECTION 64(4) OF THE 1936 ACT AND SECTION 6 OF THE 1961 ACT, AS AMENDED

Public Health Act 1936

1936 c. 49.

64.—(4) For the purposes of this Part of this Act, the expression " the prescribed period ", in relation to the passing or rejection of plans, means five weeks or such extended period (expiring not later than two months from the deposit of the plans) as may before the expiration of the five weeks be agreed in writing between the person depositing the plans and the local authority.

Public Health Act 1961

1961 c. 64.

6.—(1) Subject to the provisions of this section, if the Minister, on an application made in accordance with the provisions of this Act, considers that the operation of any requirement in building regulations would be unreasonable in relation to the particular case to which the application relates, he may, after consultation with the local authority, give a direction dispensing with or relaxing that requirement.

(2) If building regulations so provide as regards any requirement contained in the regulations, the power to dispense with or relax that requirement under subsection (1) of this section shall be exercisable by the local authority (instead of by the Minister after consultation with the local authority):

Provided that any building regulations made by virtue of this subsection may except applications of any description.

SCH. 10

(2A) If—
(a) building regulations so provide as regards any requirement contained in the regulations, and
(b) a public body considers that the operation of any such requirement would be unreasonable in relation to any particular work carried out or proposed to be carried out by or on behalf of the public body,

the public body may give a direction dispensing with or relaxing that requirement.

(2B) In subsection (2A) above " public body " means—
(a) a local authority;
(b) a county council;
(c) any other body which is prescribed for the purposes of section 52 of the Housing and Building Control Act 1984.

(3) Building regulations may provide as regards any requirement contained in the regulations that the foregoing subsections of this section shall not apply.

(4) An application under this section shall be in such form and shall contain such particulars as may be prescribed.

(5) The application shall be made to the local authority and, except where the power of giving the direction is exercisable by the local authority, the local authority shall at once transmit the application to the Minister and give notice to the applicant that it has been so transmitted.

(6) An application by a local authority in connection with a building or proposed building in the area of that authority shall be made to the Secretary of State except where the power of giving the direction is exercisable by that authority.

(7) The provisions of Part I of the First Schedule to this Act shall have effect as regards any application made under this section for a direction which will affect the application of building regulations to work which has been carried out before the making of the application.

SCHEDULE 11

Section 64.

MINOR AND CONSEQUENTIAL AMENDMENTS

Interpretation

1. In this Schedule expressions used in Part I of this Act have the same meanings as in that Part.

1967 c. 88.

The Leasehold Reform Act 1967

2.—(1) Part I of the Leasehold Reform Act 1967 (enfranchisement and extension of long leaseholds) shall not apply where, in the case of a tenancy or sub-tenancy to which this sub-paragraph applies, the landlord is a housing association and the freehold is owned by a body of persons or trust established for charitable purposes only.

SCH. 11

(2) Where a tenancy of a dwelling-house which is a house is created by the grant of a lease in pursuance of Chapter I of Part I of the 1980 Act, the tenancy shall be treated for the purposes of Part I of the said Act of 1967 as being a long tenancy notwithstanding that the lease is granted for a term not exceeding 21 years.

(3) Where a tenancy of a dwelling-house which is a house is created by the grant of a lease in pursuance of Part I of this Act, the tenancy shall be treated for the purposes of Part I of the said Act of 1967—

   (a) as being a long tenancy notwithstanding that the lease is granted for a term not exceeding 21 years ; and

   (b) as being a tenancy at a low rent notwithstanding that rent is payable under the tenancy at a yearly rate equal to or more than two-thirds of the rateable value of the dwelling-house on the first day of the term.

(4) Notwithstanding anything in sub-paragraph (3) above, where a tenancy of a dwelling-house which is a house is created by the grant of a lease in pursuance of Part I of this Act, then, so long as the rent payable under the lease exceeds £10 per annum, neither the tenant nor the tenant under a sub-tenancy directly or indirectly derived out of the tenancy shall be entitled to acquire the freehold or an extended lease of the dwelling-house under Part I of the said Act of 1967.

(5) Where, in the case of a tenancy or sub-tenancy to which this sub-paragraph applies, the tenant exercises his right to acquire the freehold under Part I of the said Act of 1967, the price payable for the dwelling-house shall be determined in accordance with section 9(1A) of that Act notwithstanding that the rateable value of the dwelling-house does not exceed £1,000 in Greater London or £500 elsewhere.

(6) Sub-paragraphs (1) and (5) above apply to—

   (a) a tenancy of a dwelling-house which is a house which is created by the grant of a lease in pursuance of Chapter I of Part I of the 1980 Act or Part I of this Act and any sub-tenancy directly or indirectly derived out of such a tenancy ; and

   (b) where in any case Part I of the said Act of 1967 applies as if there had been a single tenancy granted for a term beginning at the same time as the term under a tenancy falling within paragraph (a) above and expiring at the same time as the term under a later tenancy, that later tenancy and any sub-tenancy directly or indirectly derived out of that later tenancy ;

and sub-paragraph (5) above also applies to a tenancy which is granted in substitution for a tenancy or sub-tenancy falling within paragraph (a) or (b) above in pursuance of Part I of the said Act of 1967.

SCH. 11

1980 c. 51.

3. In section 3(1) of the said Act of 1967 (meaning of "long tenancy") in paragraph (b) of the proviso after the word "assignment" there shall be inserted the words "otherwise than by virtue of section 37A of the Housing Act 1980 (assignments by way of exchange)".

1974 c. 37.

The Health and Safety at Work etc. Act 1974

4. Subsection (3) of section 69 of the Health and Safety at Work etc. Act 1974 (appeals against certain decisions of the Secretary of State) shall be amended as follows—

(a) for paragraph (b) there shall be substituted the following paragraph—

"(b) on a reference under section 64 of the 1936 Act or section 42 of the Housing and Building Control Act 1984;";

(b) after the words "local authority", in the second place where they occur, there shall be inserted the words "or, as the case may be, the person approved for the purposes of Part II of the said Act of 1984"; and

(c) in the definition of "the relevant person" for paragraph (ii) there shall be substituted the following paragraph—

"(ii) as regards a reference under the said section 64 or the said section 42, means the person on whose application the reference was made;".

1975 c. 78.

The Airports Authority Act 1975

5. In section 19(2) of the Airports Authority Act 1975 (application of enactments relating to statutory undertakers) for the words "shall apply in relation to the Authority as it applies" there shall be substituted the words "and section 71 of that Act (which exempts such buildings from building regulations) shall apply in relation to the Authority as they apply" and for the words "(which excludes" there shall be substituted the words "and the proviso to the said section 71 (which exclude".

1980 c. 51.

The Housing Act 1980

6. Subsections (4) and (4A) of section 3 of the Housing Act 1980 (meaning of "house", "flat", "dwelling-house" etc.) shall have effect as if any reference to the right to buy included a reference to the right to be granted a shared ownership lease.

7. Section 4(3) of that Act (joint tenants and members of family occupying dwelling-house otherwise than as joint tenants) shall have effect as if the reference to Chapter I of Part I of that Act included a reference to Part I of this Act.

8.—(1) After subsection (1) of section 5 of that Act (notice claiming to exercise the right to buy) there shall be inserted the following subsection—

"(1A) A landlord's notice under subsection (1) above shall inform the tenant of any application for a determination under paragraph 5 of Part I of Schedule 1 to this Act and, in the case of a notice admitting the tenant's right, shall be without prejudice to any determination made on such an application."

SCH. 11

(2) In subsection (2) of that section for the words " three years " there shall be substituted the words " two years ".

(3) The amendment made by sub-paragraph (1) above shall not apply where the tenant's claim to exercise the right to buy was made before the coming into force of Part I of this Act; and the amendment made by sub-paragraph (2) above shall not apply where the landlord's notice under section 5(1) of that Act was served before the coming into force of Part I of this Act.

9. At the end of section 6 of that Act (purchase price) there shall be added the following subsection—

"(6) Where the secure tenant's tenancy has at any time been assigned by virtue of section 37A of this Act, the persons specified in subsection (5) above shall not include any person who under that tenancy was a secure tenant before the assignment.".

10.—(1) In subsection (1) of section 10 of that Act (notice of purchase price etc.) for the words " as soon as practicable " there shall be substituted the words " within eight weeks or, where the right is that mentioned in section 1(1)(b) above, twelve weeks ".

(2) In subsection (2) of that section for the words " section 7(5) " there shall be substituted the words " section 7(1) " and for the words " section 7(2) or (4) " there shall be substituted the words " section 7(1A), (2) or (4).".

(3) After subsection (2) of that section there shall be inserted the following subsection—

" (2A) Where the notice states provisions which would enable the landlord to recover from the tenant service charges within the meaning of Schedule 19 to this Act or section 18(1) of the 1984 Act, the notice shall also state—

(a) the landlord's estimate of the average annual amount (at current prices) which would be payable in respect of each head of charge; and

(b) the aggregate of the estimated amounts stated under paragraph (a) above;

but there shall be disregarded for the purposes of any such statement any estimated amount stated under paragraph 17 of Schedule 2 to this Act."

(4) In subsection (3) of that section after the word " mortgage ", in the first place where it occurs, there shall be inserted the words " and the effect of Part I of the 1984 Act so far as relating to the right to be granted a shared ownership lease ", for the words " section 16(4) " there shall be substituted the words " section 16(2) to (4), (6)

and (6B) " and for the word " exercising " there shall be substituted the words " claiming to exercise ".

(5) The amendments made by this paragraph shall not apply where the notice under section 10(1) of that Act was served before the coming into force of Part I of this Act.

11. In section 11(6) of that Act (right of tenant to have value determined by district valuer) for the word " exercising " there shall be substituted the words " claiming to exercise ".

12. In section 12 of that Act (claim to a mortgage) after subsection (5) there shall be inserted the following subsection—

" (5A) Where the amount which, in the opinion of the landlord or Housing Corporation, the tenant is entitled to leave outstanding, or have advanced to him, on the security of the dwelling-house is less than the aggregate mentioned in section 9(1) above, the notice shall also inform the tenant of the effect of Part I of the 1984 Act so far as relating to the right to be granted a shared ownership lease and shall be accompanied by a form for use by the tenant in claiming, in accordance with section 13(1) of that Act, that right."

13.—(1) In subsection (1) of section 13 of that Act (change of secure tenant after notice claiming right to buy) for the words from " becomes the secure tenant " to the end of paragraph (b) there shall be substituted the following paragraphs—

" (a) becomes the secure tenant under the same secure tenancy otherwise than on an assignment made by virtue of section 37A of this Act ; or

(b) becomes the secure tenant under a periodic tenancy arising by virtue of section 29 of this Act on the coming to an end of the secure tenancy ; ".

(2) In subsection (2) of that section for the word " exercising " there shall be substituted the words " claiming to exercise ".

14.—(1) Section 18 of that Act (right to a mortgage—terms of mortgage deed) shall have effect as if any reference to the deed by which a mortgage is effected in pursuance of Chapter I of Part I of that Act included a reference to the deed by which a further mortgage is effected in pursuance of section 16 of this Act.

(2) Where that section applies in relation to such a deed by virtue of sub-paragraph (1) above, it shall also have effect as if any reference to the term of a lease were a reference to the unexpired term of that lease.

15.—(1) Section 19 of that Act (dwelling-houses in National Parks and areas of outstanding natural beauty etc.) shall have effect as if any reference to Chapter I of Part I of that Act included a reference to Part I of this Act.

(2) Where that section applies in relation to the grant of a shared ownership lease by virtue of sub-paragraph (1) above, it shall also have effect as if—

    (a) in subsections (2), (4) and (12) for the words " section 8(3A) of this Act " there were substituted the words " paragraph 6(5) of Schedule 3 to the 1984 Act " ;

    (b) in subsection (6) for the words " section 8(1) of this Act " there were substituted the words " paragraph 6(1) or 7(1) of Schedule 3 to the 1984 Act " ;

    (c) in subsection (7) for the words " subsection (3A) of section 8 of this Act " there were substituted the words " sub-paragraph (5) of paragraph 6 of Schedule 3 to the 1984 Act " and for the words " subsection (1) of that section " there were substituted the words " sub-paragraph (1) of that paragraph or paragraph 7(1) of that Schedule " ;

    (d) in subsection (11) for the words " section 8(3A)(d) or (e) of this Act " there were substituted the words " paragraph 6(5)(d) or (e) of Schedule 3 to the 1984 Act " ; and

    (e) in subsection (12), in the definition of " relevant disposal " for the words " section 8 of this Act " there were substituted the words " paragraph 6 of Schedule 3 to the 1984 Act."

16. Section 20 of that Act (registration of title) shall have effect as if—

    (a) the reference to the conveyance of a freehold in pursuance of Chapter I of Part I of that Act included a reference to the conveyance of a freehold in pursuance of such a right as is mentioned in paragraph 3(5) or 7(5) of Schedule 3 to this Act ; and

    (b) the reference to the grant of a lease in pursuance of that Chapter included a reference to the grant of a lease in pursuance of Part I of this Act.

17.—(1) For section 21 of that Act (costs) there shall be substituted the following section—

"Costs.

21.—(1) Any agreement between—

    (a) a tenant claiming to exercise the right to buy and the landlord ; or

    (b) a tenant claiming to exercise the right to a mortgage and the landlord or, as the case may be, the Housing Corporation,

shall be void in so far as it purports to oblige the tenant to bear any part of the costs incurred by the landlord or Housing Corporation in connection with the tenant's exercise of that right.

(2) Where a tenant exercises the right to a mortgage, the landlord or, as the case may be, the Housing Corporation may charge to him the costs incurred by it in connection with the tenant's exercise of that right, but only on the execution of the deed by which the mortgage is effected and to the extent that those costs do not exceed such amount as the Secretary of State may by order specify."

SCH. 11

(2) That section as so substituted shall have effect as if—

(a) the reference to the right to buy included a reference to the right to be granted a shared ownership lease and to such rights as are mentioned in paragraphs 3(1) and (5) and 7(5) of Schedule 3 to this Act ; and

(b) the reference to the right to a mortgage included a reference to such a right as is mentioned in section 16(1) of this Act.

18.—(1) After subsection (1) of section 22 of that Act (notices) there shall be inserted the following subsection—

"(1A) Where the form of and the particulars to be contained in a notice under this Chapter are so prescribed a tenant who proposes to claim or has claimed to exercise the right to buy may request the landlord to supply him with a form for use in giving such a notice, and the landlord shall do so within seven days of the request."

(2) That section shall have effect as if any reference to Chapter I of Part I of that Act included a reference to Part I of this Act.

19.—(1) Subsection (5) of section 23 of that Act (Secretary of State's power to intervene) shall be omitted.

(2) In subsection (9) of that section for the words " on demand " onwards there shall be substituted the words " on a date specified in the certificate, together with interest from that date at a rate so specified ".

(3) In subsection (11) of that section for the words " subsections (5) to (10) " there shall be substituted the words " subsections (6) to (10) ".

(4) That section shall have effect as if any reference to Chapter I of Part I of that Act included a reference to Part I of this Act and any reference to the right to buy included a reference to the right to be granted a shared ownership lease.

20.—(1) In subsection (2) of section 24 of that Act (vesting orders) for the words " the landlord and the tenant and their successors in title " there shall be substituted the words " both the landlord and its successors in title and the tenant and his successors in title (including any person deriving title under him or them) ".

(2) That section shall have effect as if any reference to Chapter I of Part I of that Act included a reference to Part I of this Act.

21. The following provisions of that Act, namely—

section 24A (Secretary of State's power to give directions as to covenants and conditions) ;
- section 24B (effect of directions on existing covenants and conditions) ;
section 24C (Secretary of State's power to obtain information etc.) ;
section 24D (Secretary of State's power to give assistance) ; and
section 25 (statutory declarations),

shall have effect as if any reference to Chapter I of Part I of that Act included a reference to Part I of this Act and any reference to the right to buy included a reference to the right to be granted a shared ownership lease.

SCH. 11

22. In section 27(3) of that Act (interpretation of Chapter I), for the words "Chapter II", in the first place where they occur, there shall be substituted the words "Part I of the 1984 Act", after the words "Chapter II", in the second place where they occur, there shall be inserted the words "and that Part" and for paragraphs (a) and (b) there shall be substituted the following paragraphs—

"(a) a predecessor of a local authority within the definition in section 50(1) shall be deemed to have been such an authority;

(b) a predecessor of a county council shall be deemed to have been such a council; and

(c) a housing association shall be deemed to have been registered under Part II of the 1974 Act if it is or was so registered at any later time".

23. In subsection (1) of section 31 of that Act (meaning of successor) for the words from "but a tenant" onwards there shall be substituted the words "but subject to subsection (1A) below" and after that subsection there shall be inserted the following subsection—

"(1A) A tenant to whom the tenancy was assigned in pursuance of an order under section 24 of the Matrimonial Causes Act 1973 is a successor only if the other party to the marriage was himself a successor; and a tenant to whom the tenancy was assigned by virtue of section 37A below is a successor only if he was a successor in relation to the tenancy which he himself assigned by virtue of that section.".

1973 c. 18.

24. In section 50(1) of that Act (interpretation of Chapter II of Part I) immediately before the definition of "development corporation" there shall be inserted the following definition—

"'cemetery' has the same meaning as in section 214 of the Local Government Act 1972;".

1972 c. 70.

25.—(1) In subsection (2) of section 86 of that Act (jurisdiction of county court and rules of procedure) there shall be inserted after paragraph (a) the following paragraph—

"(aa) whether any consent required by section 37A was withheld otherwise than on one or more of the grounds set out in Schedule 4A to this Act;".

(2) That section shall have effect as if any reference to any question arising under Part I of that Act or Chapter I of Part I of that Act included a reference to any question arising under Part I of this Act or any lease granted in pursuance of it.

26. In section 110(1) of that Act (local authority mortgage interest rates) at the end of paragraph (c) there shall be inserted the words "or section 20 of the 1984 Act".

27. In subsection (1) of section 127 of that Act (registration of housing associations) for the words from the beginning to " its objects " there shall be substituted the words " Section 13 of the 1974 Act (the register of housing associations) shall have effect as if the additional purposes or objects mentioned in subsection (3) of that section included " and the words from " without " onwards shall be omitted.

28. In section 137(1) of that Act (avoidance of certain unauthorised disposals) after the words " section 128(2) of the Local Government Act 1972 " there shall be inserted the words ", section 29 of the Town and Country Planning Act 1959 ".

29. At the end of section 150 of that Act (interpretation) there shall be inserted the following definition—

" ' the 1984 Act ' means the Housing and Building Control Act 1984 ".

30. In section 151(1) of that Act (regulations and orders) after the word " section ", in the second place where it occurs, there shall be inserted the word " 8(5) ".

31. Part II of Schedule 1A to that Act (qualification and discount) shall have effect as if " previous discount " included a discount which was given, before the relevant time, in pursuance of the provision required by paragraph 3 of Schedule 3 to this Act or any other provision to the like effect.

32. Part IV of Schedule 2 to that Act (charges and other matters) shall have effect as if any reference to the right to buy included a reference to the right to be granted a shared ownership lease and to such rights as are mentioned in paragraphs 3(5) and 7(5) of Schedule 3 to this Act.

33.—(1) Paragraph 1 of Schedule 3 to that Act (tenancies which are not secure tenancies) shall have effect as if the reference to a tenancy granted in pursuance of Chapter I of Part I of that Act included a reference to a tenancy granted in pursuance . Part I of this Act.

(2) In paragraph 2(1) of that Schedule for paragraphs (*a*) to (*e*) there shall be substituted the words " a body specified in paragraph 1(3) of Schedule 1 to this Act ".

(3) In paragraph 8 of that Schedule for the words " or his predecessor in title ", in the first place where they occur, there shall be substituted the words " (or a predecessor in title of his) " and for the words " (or his predecessor in title) ", in the second place where they occur, there shall be substituted the words " or predecessor ".

34. In Part I of Schedule 4 to that Act, in ground 6, for the words " or his predecessor in title ", in the first place where they occur, there shall be substituted the words " (or a predecessor in title of his) " and for the words " he (or his predecessor in title) ", in both places where they occur, there shall be substituted the words " the tenant or predecessor ".

The Civil Aviation Act 1982   SCH. 11

35. In paragraph 1(1) of Schedule 2 to the Civil Aviation Act 1982 1982 c. 16. (application of enactments relating to statutory undertakers etc.) for the words " shall apply in relation to the CAA as it applies " there shall be substituted the words " and section 71 of that Act (which exempts such buildings from building regulations) shall apply in relation to the CAA as they apply " and for the words " (which excludes " there shall be substituted the words " and the proviso to the said section 71 (which exclude ".

SCHEDULE 12

Sections 61 and 65.

REPEALS

PART I

REPEALS RELATING TO BUILDING CONTROL

Chapter	Short title	Extent of repeal
1966 c. 27.	The Building Control Act 1966.	The whole Act.
1966 c. 34.	The Industrial Development Act 1966.	In Schedule 3, Part I.
1968 c. 73.	The Transport Act 1968.	In Schedule 16, paragraph 9.
1969 c. 35.	The Transport (London) Act 1969.	In Schedule 3, paragraph 9(2)(*a*).
1969 c. 48.	The Post Office Act 1969.	In Schedule 4, paragraph 80.
1971 c. 78.	The Town and Country Planning Act 1971.	In Schedule 23, in Part II, the entry relating to the Building Control Act 1966.
1972 c. 5.	The Local Employment Act 1972.	In Schedule 3, the entry relating to the Building Control Act 1966.
1972 c. 52.	The Town and Country Planning (Scotland) Act 1972.	In Schedule 21, in Part II, the entry relating to the Building Control Act 1966.
1975 c. 64.	The Iron and Steel Act 1975.	In Schedule 6, paragraph 7.
1977 c. 49.	The National Health Service Act 1977.	In Schedule 14, in paragraph 13(1)(*b*), the words " 107 to ". In Schedule 15, paragraph 38.
1978 c. 44.	The Employment Protection (Consolidation) Act 1978.	In Schedule 16, paragraph 32.
1981 c. 38.	The British Telecommunications Act 1981.	In Schedule 3, paragraph 45.

PART II

FURTHER REPEALS

Chapter	Short title	Extent of repeal
26 Geo. 5 & 1 Edw. 8. c. 49.	The Public Health Act 1936.	Section 67.
5 & 6 Eliz. 2. c. 56.	The Housing Act 1957.	Section 104C(4).

Sch. 12

Chapter	Short title	Extent of repeal
1974 c. 37.	The Health and Safety at Work etc. Act 1974.	Section 61(5). Section 62(3). Section 63(6) and (7). In section 69, in subsection (1) the words " section 64 of the 1936 Act ". In Schedule 6, in Part I, paragraphs 1, 2, sub-paragraphs (*a*), (*d*) and (*e*) of paragraph 5, and paragraphs 6 and 7, and Part II except in so far as it sets out section 4 of the Public Health Act 1961. In Schedule 10, in the third column of the entry relating to the Public Health Act 1936, the words " Section 71 ", the entry relating to the Education Act 1944 and, in the third column of the entry relating to the Public Health Act 1961, the words " Section 7(3) to (6) ", " Section 10(1) and (2) " and " and 71 ".
1975 c. 78.	The Airports Authority Act 1975.	Section 25(10).
1980 c. 51.	The Housing Act 1980.	In section 2, in subsection (4) the words " Subject to subsection (5) below " and subsection (5). In section 7, subsections (5) to (11). Section 15. In section 18(1), the words from " but the Secretary of State " onwards. Section 19(8). Section 23(5). In section 24, in subsections (3) and (5) the word " land ". In section 28(2), paragraph (*d*) and the word " or " immediately preceding that paragraph. In section 127(1), the words from " without " onwards. In Schedule 2, in the provision renumbered as paragraph 15(1), paragraph (*b*) and the words " and paragraph 16 below ". In Schedule 3, paragraph 3.
1980 c. 65.	The Local Government, Planning and Land Act 1980.	In section 156, subsection (1) and in subsection (2)(*b*), the words from " and " onwards.

SCH. 12

1. The repeal of section 2(5) of the Housing Act 1980 has effect subject to section 2(4) of this Act.

2. The repeals of sections 7(5) to (11) and 15 of that Act have effect subject to section 3(6) of this Act.

PRINTED IN ENGLAND BY W. J. SHARP
Controller and Chief Executive of Her Majesty's Stationery Office and
Queen's Printer of Acts of Parliament